The Secrets, Mysteries & Powers of The Subconscious Mind

Compiled and Edited
by
David Allen

Copyright © 2017

Copyright © 2017 by Shanon Allen / David Allen

All rights reserved. No part of this publication may be reproduced, distributed, or transmitted in any form or by any means, including photocopying, recording, or other electronic or mechanical methods, without the prior written permission of the publisher, except in the case of brief quotations embodied in critical reviews and certain other noncommercial uses permitted by copyright law. Printed in the United States of America

First Paperback Edition, April 2017

ISBN: 978-0-9972801-9-7

Visit Us At **NevilleGoddardBooks.com** for a complete listing of all our books and **1000's of Free Books to Read online and download.**

Introduction

This volume contains several chapters from various law of attraction/metaphysical books of the last 100 years. As with all my compilations I have taken what I consider to be some of the best information from some of the best books and compiled it into one book, without what I would consider filler in many books, leaving only the gold, such as I AM, Imagination, Inner Conversations, Thought and so on.

The introduction below is from Joseph Murphy's, The Power of The Subconscious Mind, which I feel is very fitting for this volume.

Infinite riches are all around you if you will open your mental eyes and behold the treasure house of infinity within you. There is a gold mine within you from which you can extract everything you need to live life gloriously, joyously, and abundantly. Many are sound asleep because they do not know about this gold mine of infinite intelligence and boundless love within themselves. Whatever you want, you can draw forth. A magnetized piece of steel will lift about twelve times its own weight, and if you demagnetize this same piece of steel, it will not even lift a feather. Similarly, there are two types of men. There is the magnetized man who is full of confidence and faith. He knows that he is born to win and to succeed. Then, there is the type of man who is demagnetized. He is full of fears and doubts. Opportunities come, and he says, "I might fail; I might lose my money; people will laugh at me." This type of man will not get very far in life because, if he is afraid to go forward, he will simply stay where he is. Become a magnetized man and discover the master secret of the ages.

What, in your opinion, is the master secret of the ages? The secret of atomic energy? Thermonuclear energy? The neutron bomb? Interplanetary travel? No .. not any of these. Then, what is this master secret? Where can one find it, and how can it be contacted and brought into action? The answer is extraordinarily simple. This secret is the marvelous, miracle-working power found in your own subconscious mind, the last place that most people would seek it.

You can bring into your life more power, more wealth, more health, more happiness, and more joy by learning to contact and release the hidden power of your subconscious mind. You need not acquire this power; you already possess it. But, you want to learn how to use it; you want to understand it so that you can apply it in all departments of your life.

Within your subconscious depths lie infinite wisdom, infinite power, and infinite supply of all that is necessary, which is waiting for development and expression. Begin now to recognize these potentialities of your deeper mind, and they will take form in the world without.

Foreword

Learn about the Secrets, Mysteries and Powers of your Deeper Mind from some of the best metaphysical authors of the last 100 years. Authors include Orison Swett Marden, Julia Seton Sears, Kate Atkinson Boehme, Louis E. Bisch, Henry Thomas Hamblin, Eugene Del Mar, Elsie Lincoln Benedict, Christian Larson, Abel Leighton Allen, Charles M. Simmons, Thomas Parker Boyd, Charles F. Winbigler, Neville Goddard, W. John Murray, Venice Bloodworth, Paul C. Ferrell, Robert Collier, U.S. Andersen, Charles F. Haanel, Charles W. McCrossan, Bruce MacLelland.

While many authors didn't devote an entire book to the subconscious mind, they did devote at least a chapter to it. This book is a compilation of those very chapters.

David Allen

Table of Contents

Chapter 1 - Chapter XI of Orison Swett Marden's "Prosperity: How To Attract It" (1922) How to make your subconscious mind work for you - Page 11

Chapter 2 - Chapter IV of Julia Seton Sears' "The Psychology Of The Solar Plexus and Subconscious Mind" (1914) The Subconscious Mind - Page 22

Chapter 3 - Chapter III of Kate Atkinson Boehme's "New Thought Healing Made Plain" (1918) The Subconscious Mind - Page 30

Chapter 4 - Chapter I of Louis E. Bisch's "Your Inner Self" (1922) The Inner Self - The Unconscious or the Subconscious - Page 40

Chapter 5 - Chapter VIII of Henry Thomas Hamblin's "Within You is the Power" (1920) The Powers and The Limitations of The Subconscious Mind - Page 46

Chapter 6 - Chapter XI of Eugene Del Mar's "The Conquest of Disease" (1922) Conscious and Subconscious - Page 52

Chapter 7 - Elsie Lincoln Benedict's "How to Unlock Your Subconscious Mind Through the Science of Mental Analysis" (1922) Your Secret, Subconscious Self - Page 59

Chapter 8 - Chapter IV of Christian Larson's "Your Forces And How To Use Them" (1912) The Forces of the Subconscious - Page 80

Chapter 9 - Chapter IV of Christian Larson's "Your Forces And How To Use Them" (1912) Training The Subconscious for Practical Results - Page 91

Chapter 10 - Chapter VI of Christian D. Larson's "How To Stay Young" (1906) Training the Subconscious to Produce Perpetually the Elements of Youth - Page 99

Chapter 11 - Chapter VIII of Abel Leighton Allen's "The Message of New Thought" (1914) As A Man Thinketh - Page 109

Chapter 12 - Excerpt from Chapter V of Abel Leighton Allen's "The Message of New Thought" (1914) Universal Mind in Man - Page 119

Chapter 13 - Chapter XIII of Charles M. Simmons "Your Subconscious Power, How To Make It Work For You" (1957) How to Use the Power of Your Subconscious - Page 121

Chapter 14 - Chapter III of Thomas Parker Boyd's "The Mental Highway" (1922) Conscious, Subconscious and Superconscious - Page 129

Chapter 15 - Chapter III of Charles F. Winbigler's "Suggestion, its Law and Application, or, The Principal and Practice of Psycho-Therapeutics" (1919) The Relation of Suggestion to the Subconscious Mind - Page 134

Chapter 16 - Chapter I of Neville Goddard's "Feeling is the Secret" (1944) Law and its Operation - Page 143

Chapter 17 - Chapter VII of W. John Murray's "Mental Medicine" (1923) The Subconscious Mind - Page 151

Chapter 18 - Chapter IV of Venice Bloodworth's "Key To Yourself" (1952) The Subconscious Mind - Page 156

Chapter 19 - Chapter II of Paul C. Ferrell's - "The Subconscious Speaks" (1932) Using Conscious Thought in a Definitely Creative Manner - Page 159

Chapter 20 - A Few Excerpts From Various Metaphysical Authors on The Subconscious Mind - Page 166

Christian Larson's "The Great Within" (Complete Book) (1907) - Page 180

Metaphysical/Law of Attraction Books by David Allen - Page - 259

Notes - 260 - 261

THE most fundamental and the most far reaching activity in life is that which you build into your mentality every waking hour. Your word is silent and invisible; nevertheless, it is real.

You are building your mental home all the time, and your thought and mental imagery represent your blueprint. Hour by hour, moment by moment, you can build radiant health, success, and happiness by the thoughts you think, the ideas which you harbor, the beliefs that you accept, and the scenes that you rehearse in the hidden studio of your mind. This stately mansion, upon the construction of which you are perpetually engaged, is your personality, your identity in this plane, your whole life story on this earth.

Get a new blueprint; build silently by realizing peace, harmony, joy, and good will in the present moment. By dwelling upon these things and claiming them, your subconscious will accept your blueprint and bring all these things to pass. By their fruits ye shall know them.

Joseph Murphy

Chapter 1

Chapter XI

of

Orison Swett Marden's "Prosperity: How To Attract It"

(1922)

How To Make Your Subconscious Mind Work For You

- When all men know how to make the subconscious work for them there will be no poor people, none in distress or suffering, in pain or ill health; no one will be unhappy, no one will be a victim of thwarted ambitions.

- Your subconscious mind is like a garden, and you must be very careful what you plant there. Every thought, every emotion, every suggestion is a seed planted in the subconscious soil, and will bring you a harvest like itself. It doesn't matter what kind of thought seeds you plant, whether poverty or prosperity, failure or success, happiness or misery, you will reap a harvest in kind.

- If you impress vividly, intensely, and persistently, upon the creative mind in the great within of you, your determination to be what you long to be; if you register your vow to succeed in doing what you long to do; and do your level best to actualize your longings, nothing in the world can stand in the way of your success.

- Every great inventor, every great discoverer, every great genius has felt the thrill of the divine inward force, that mysterious power back of the flesh but not of it, which has come to his aid in working out the device, the discovery, the book, the painting, the great musical composition, the poem, whatever he was trying to create or discover.

I predict that within the next twenty-five years the average man, through his knowledge of the infinite power and possibilities of the subconscious mind, that mysterious force in the great within, will be able to accomplish more than the greatest minds of all time have ever dreamed of doing.

Science has revealed the mechanism of the body and mastered the secrets of its marvelous construction and action; but the mystery of mind is as yet but dimly understood. Very few have even a faint realization of its immense hidden powers.

The body becomes unconscious in sleep and all its voluntary activities cease. But the mind . . what does it do when the body sleeps? We know it does not sleep, for when the body is wrapped in slumber the memory and imagination slip out of their house and go where they will. They wander in scenes of the past or they project themselves into the future.

Now they are visiting in California, now in London, now in Paris, now they are among the stars. What embodiment do they assume? Or do they take visible form? They certainly seem to be completely independent of the body during sleep. The new psychology explains the mystery of mind in a very simple way. It claims that that part of the mind which continues active when we sleep is that marvelous force in the great within of us which, understood and rightly used, will enable man to reach the heights of his limitless possibilities.

We know that we are tapping a new source of power. When we can do this intelligently, scientifically, we shall all be performing what hitherto have been regarded as miracles. We are just beginning to realize that the subconscious mind is the channel by which we connect with infinite supply; with the great creative processes of the universe; that through it man can tap the Infinite Mind and accomplish things that will dwarf to insignificance achievements that now excite our wonder and admiration.

Everything, so far as results are concerned, depends upon the degree of intelligence and conscious purpose with which we use the subconscious mind, for it is forever occupied registering on the invisible creative substance your every thought, emotion, desire, wish, or feeling. It never sleeps, but is incessantly working on the suggestions it receives from the conscious or objective mind. Your habitual thought, your convictions, your visions, your dreams, your beliefs, are all impressed upon it, and will ultimately be expressed in your life.

In other words, your subconscious mind is your servant, and proceeds instantly, without quibbling, without questioning, no matter whether it is a big thing or a little thing, whether it is right or wrong, to obey the order, to follow the suggestion, you give it.

For instance, when you want to take an early train, or to get up in the middle of the night for some purpose, when you haven't been accustomed to do so, and you say to yourself, or hold the thought in mind before dropping to sleep, "I must wake up in time to get that train in the morning," or, "I must get up at one o'clock tonight," you are sure to awaken at almost the exact time you register, when, perhaps, you haven't been awake at that hour before in a year. You have no alarm clock; no one calls you; what wakes you up at just the right time? You probably never asked yourself the question, or thought about it. But it was that little faithful subconscious servant who was on the watch for you while you slept.

A similar thing is true of our appointments; making dates or engagements for some time in the future. You agree to meet a man tomorrow or someday next week at a certain place and hour. You don't make any written record of it and the thing passes out of your mind. But when the time comes round you are reminded of your engagement. From long experience I know that that something inside of me will bring every engagement I make to my consciousness in time for me to attend to it. I don't keep thinking of it all the time. Not at all. I file it away in the within of me as I would file a business letter in my office for future reference. Then I dismiss it from my thought, knowing that it will be taken care of at the proper time.

The trained man learns to commit all sorts of things to his subconscious secretary, knowing from experience that it will serve him faithfully, not only in comparatively small things, such as awakening him at any desired hour in the night or early morning, constantly reminding him of his engagements, but also in the serious problems of life. Edison says that when he is right up against a great problem in his work and has no idea in the world how to solve it, he simply sleeps over it, and many a time he wakes up in the morning to find his problem solved; it has been worked out for him while he slept in ways which he never dreamed of. The details of various inventions have been completed for him in this way.

I know a great many business and professional men who do as Mr. Edison does when serious problems confront them; they sleep on them before they make any decision. In fact, it is the commonest thing in the world, when we are considering some serious problem, for all of us to say: "I must sleep over that matter before deciding; it is so important." What does sleeping over such a matter mean? We may not understand or be able to explain, but what it really means is this: Your subconscious mind takes up the problem at the point where your conscious mind left it when you went to sleep, and in the morning you will find that it has been thought out for you. Your subconscious wisdom has entered into the transaction, given you the benefit of its advice and enabled you to make the right decision.

When all men know how to make the subconscious work for them there will be no poor people, none in distress or suffering, in pain or ill health; no one will be unhappy, a victim of thwarted ambitions. We shall know then that all we have to do to make our dreams come true, to be prosperous and happy, is to give our invisible secretary the right instructions and follow this up with the necessary effort.

Establishing in your subconscious mind the things that you want to come true, that you are ambitious to attain; impressing upon it the ideal of the man or woman you long to be, is the first step toward achievement. Hold the conviction in your consciousness that your own is already headed your way, work for it confidently in the realization that you can draw from the creative energy of the universal mind anything you desire, and it will surely come to you, because you will thus start the process of creation in the great within of you.

Consciously or unconsciously put in motion, these are the initial steps that have led to the production of every great work of art and genius in the world. They were adopted in the production of our railroads, our ships, our homes, our great monuments and buildings, our cities, our telegraph, telephone, and wireless systems, our airplanes, and all the marvels of modern inventions. Edison says he is only a medium for transmitting from the great cosmic intelligence and energy which fill the universe a few of the infinite number of devices which are destined to emancipate human beings from every form of drudgery. He believes that the best things he has given to the world have been merely passed along through him to his fellow men from the Infinite Source of all supply.

While the subconscious mind is all-powerful in working out the pattern or idea we give it, of itself it does not originate, so it will make all the difference in the world to you what sort of material you give your subconscious mind to work on.

You can make it an enemy or a friend, for it will do the thing which injures you just as quickly as the thing which blesses you. Not through malice, but because it has no discriminating power any more than the soil in which the farmer sows his seed. If the farmer should make a mistake and sow thistle seed instead of wheat, the soil doesn't say to him, "My friend, you have made a mistake. You have been sowing thistle seed instead of wheat, so we will change the law, which you may get what you thought you were going to get." No, the soil will always give us a harvest like our sowing.

If we sow thistle seed it will be just as faithful in producing thistles as it will in producing wheat or cabbages or potatoes. We sow the seed and nature gives us a corresponding harvest; that is the law on the physical plane. It is exactly the same on the mental plane. The subconscious mind is like the soil, passive. The objective mind uses it, gives its commands or suggestions, which it carries out according to their nature. That is, the objective or conscious mind sows the seed in word, motive, thought or act, and the subconscious mind gives us back our own; always the thing that corresponds to what we impressed on it.

In other words, the subconscious mind has no choice but to follow the lead we give it. Hence, how important it is that our instructions to this invisible servant should be for our good and not for our harm; that we should saturate it, not with the things we do not want, the things we hate and fear and worry about, but the things we long for and are striving to attain.

If you are working hard, and yet not progressing toward your ideal; if you are in poverty and wretchedness, though constantly struggling to get away from those conditions; you are not obeying the law "which governs the subconscious. Your thought is at fault; you are thinking poverty, thinking failure; your mind is filled with doubts and fears; you are working against the law instead of with it; you are neutralizing all your efforts by your wrong mental attitude.

Some people by their indomitable faith and self-confidence get hold of the dormant powers of the great within of themselves and unconsciously work with the law which governs them. Wherever a man or a woman is doing unusual things, struggling heroically to accomplish some great purpose, you find one who consciously or unconsciously is obeying this law, by making tremendous demands upon the subconscious; by registering his life purposes with such tremendous intensity and working so persistently, so confidently, along that line that his purpose is unfailingly carried out. Luther Burbank, for example, has done and is doing tremendous things in the plant world because he makes tremendous demands upon the mighty agent within, his subconscious mind or self.

He does not neutralize the demands by doubts and fears as to whether they will be carried out or not. He makes his demands, gives his orders, persistently, emphatically, with vigor and determination, and they are faithfully executed. By the same means, consciously or unconsciously used, Madam Curie has made some of the most remarkable discoveries in the scientific world. We can all accomplish our ends, attain our life ambition by doing as they and all other great achievers are doing . . working with law. We are not, as we were taught to believe in the past, so many separate little bits of mind thrown off into space to struggle for ourselves; we are all a part of the infinite mind, the cosmic intelligence and energy of the universe.

We are the creation of the one Supreme Mind which called all things out of the unseen, and since the created must partake of the qualities of the Creator, man must partake of the qualities of omniscience, of omnipotence, of the Supreme Mind that gave man dominion over the earth and everything on it. This means that we are really, so far as this earth is concerned, in partnership with God, that we are co-creators with the great creative intelligence which is everywhere active in the universe.

The marvelous accomplishments of man within the past few centuries can only be accounted for through his cooperation with his Creator. It is the spirit of God in man working in harmony with the spirit of God in the great cosmic intelligence of the universe which has made possible within the past half century achievements in science, in invention, in discovery that our ancestors would have ridiculed . . if anyone dared to suggest them as possibilities . . as the imaginings of the insane.

The Secrets, Mysteries & Powers of The Subconscious Mind

Wireless telegraphy and telephony, the automobile, the airplane; the harnessing of electricity to do the work in our factories, in our homes; the reconstruction of the body by great surgeons, the discoveries in astronomy; cables under oceans, connecting the ends of the earth; the construction of railroads under rivers and under the streets of our teeming cities; the works of scientific men in every field, of the great agriculturists, horticulturists and naturalists, and the great animal breeders who are doing in the animal world what the Burbanks are doing in the plant world . . all these things are the results of man's reaching out into the great creative energy and in cooperation with Omnipotence molding it to his purposes.

The dictum of science is that "Nature unaided fails." In other words, man is God's working partner on this earth, his work being to lift everything upon it, including man himself, to the highest possibility of the divine plan. There is a power in man back of the flesh, which, working with the divine cosmic intelligence, will enable him to do things that at present we can hardly conceive of. Nothing we can imagine or dream" of will be impossible of achievement, because we are a real part of the creative power which performs miracles throughout the universe. That is, apparent miracles, for everything follows a law which is never violated in order to perform what seem to us miracles.

In the consciousness of the mighty possibilities of the subconscious mind to tap the great universal mind lies the secret of infinite creative principle, of limitless power. There are powers in your subconscious mind which, if aroused and utilized, would help you do what others tell you is "impossible." Your ideal, your heart's desire, however unattainable it may seem at present, is a prophecy of what will come true in your life if you do your part. It is only in our extremities that we touch our real power, that we unconsciously have recourse to the great within. There are multitudes of people in the failure army today, with scarcely energy enough to keep them alive, who have forces slumbering deep within themselves which, if they could only be awakened, would enable them to do wonderful things.

The great trouble with most of us, even those who have studied along this line, is that our demands upon ourselves are so feeble, the call upon the great within of us is so weak and so intermittent, that it makes no vital or permanent impression upon the creative energies; it lacks the force and persistency that transmute desires into realities. When we realize that it is through our subconscious selves, in the great within of us, that we make wireless connection with the All-Supply, with all possible joy and satisfaction; that it is here the great creative processes which make our dreams come true are started, it seems strange that we don't use this great force to better advantage.

When the necessary conditions are fulfilled the law that governs the subconscious operates unerringly. Work with the law instead of against it and nothing can hinder your success. In other words, let your subconscious mind help instead of hinder you.

Give it the right thought, the right instruction, the right ideals to work on; give it success thoughts instead of failure thoughts, bright cheerful, hopeful thoughts instead of gloomy discouraging ones; never hold a thought that does not correspond with your ideal or ambition; no matter what conditions are, what obstacles stand in your way, persist in vividly visualizing your success, never letting a doubt or fear thought come between you and the confident belief that you will get the thing you long for and are working for with all your heart, and you will be amazed at what your faithful secretary, working in harmony with creative intelligence, will do for you.

The interior creative forces are more active during the night than in the day time, and are especially susceptible to the suggestions they receive before we fall asleep. During sleep the conscious mind is not active, and consequently the subconscious mind operates uninterruptedly, without any of the objections or hindrances which it is constantly bringing up during the day.

Therefore it is of the greatest importance that you give the subconscious the right message, the right model on which to work during the night. Do this before you drop to sleep and it will work for the attainment of your ambition, your desire, all night. Never allow yourself to fall asleep in a doubting, despondent mood.

Do not hinder the operation of the creative intelligence at any time by doubt, or fear. Doubt is the great enemy which has neutralized the efforts, and killed the success of multitudes of people. Live always in the consciousness that you are a success in whatever you are trying to do and the creative processes within you, faithfully working according to the model you give them, will produce whatever you desire.

Chapter 2

Chapter IV

of

Julia Seton Sears' "The Psychology Of The Solar Plexus and Subconscious Mind"

(1914)

The Subconscious Mind

THERE have been so many things written about the subconscious mind, its use and power, that the student must wander in a maze of uncertainty and confusion unless he can be turned back into the straight path of research.

It is time for higher revelation on this subject, and today there are those who know more clearly the great truths which the earlier psychologists only dimly foreshadowed. It is the task of the twentieth century mystics to offer a clearer interpretation than has hitherto been given.

The first psychologists taught that man possessed an objective side of consciousness and held the subjective side to be endowed with greater power than the objective, but they threw little light on what these two states of consciousness meant. From these earlier teachings there has evolved the practice in the new thought world of hobnobbing with one's own subjective mind rather than getting into union with the One Mind.

We were told that suggestion to our sub-self or subconscious mind would bring about within us certain well-defined experiences; so while the old thought world prayed to its Jesus, the new thought world suggested to its subconsciousness.

It is plain to those seeking to scientifically understand life's finer forces, that there are some very finely marked laws in operation, and we cannot go very far in investigation until we find there are many states of consciousness within us with which the ordinary individual is entirely unfamiliar, and following this clue we come face to face with the fundamentals of universal mind.

The psychologists of today see only one substance, and find this substance is formed from minute atoms, each atom possessing its own intelligence or atomic mind.

Man is the highest point of localized atoms, and he and his environment become a well-marked center of activity within the larger universal world-mind.

Man's physical body is only a combination of atoms attuned to move at its own vibratory rate, the outer substance is simply a shell, composed of separate points of intelligence.

Mind is always clothed in body and the central undifferentiated atomic stream of intelligence within us is called our Spirit, while the outer crusts of this differentiated substance are called body, but they are really one substance.

There must always be the outside and inside action of every law, so there is no such thing as a body and a spirit . . there is only the outside and inside action of universal mind.

Our physical cell body is a crust of atomic intelligence, and is endowed with a brain, nerve centers and system of nerves through which the spirit or higher intelligence can play, and within this physical body is another body of much finer substance because it is much more vibrant; and within this finer body or second is a third body of still finer substance, and so on . . each body in turn holding another body, reaching the seventh dimension. There are three bodies with which individuals in the ordinary consciousness become familiar; the others belong to the fourth, fifth, sixth and seventh dimensions of consciousness and only a few on this planet are awake in these states of vibration.

Each body is endowed with its centers for expression, and these centers correlate with the brain and nervous centers of the physical body, and when the physical body is polarized and functioning normally, it receives, sends out, is vitalized and sustained by the energy of the finer etheric intelligence of its inner bodies. Combined with the cell intelligence these bodies are linked into one by the central intelligence within them, or the one mind.

Each body is distinct in itself, yet no one can say, " here one begins," or, " here one ends," for they interpenetrate as water does among the grains of sand; the atoms of each body are held in suspension within the fluidic substance of the other bodies.

These bodies can be separated and passed out at will by those who know the law, and each one is powerful on the plane with which it has correspondence, and when we know how to manipulate the physical body and its cell consciousness through the consciousness of the other bodies, we produce within the physical body a law of life of which those who are working only with the intelligence of the physical consciousness know nothing.

These bodies are held together centralized into one point in the solar plexus of the physical side. What the older psychologists fondly called the subconscious mind is nothing but the inner second body and its accompanying state of consciousness. This body is called by those who name it the "psychic self." When one can function in this part of his consciousness and has become acquainted with this self, he is more powerful in his physical body. Suggestions to the subconscious mind did this much good . . they vitalized the activity of the psychic mind and body and rendered more possible its power to manifest through the physical self, for, while suggesting, the student was, to a small degree, suspending operation of his lower state of consciousness, or his physical objective mind, giving more positive expression to his finer forces. The psychic body manifests through the centers of the physical brain; the solar plexus, with the higher concept centers of the physical brain, acting as the switchboard where connection is made for consciousness, holds all force intact.

All the diseases of the world, except accidental wounds, fractures and septic infection, are simply the discordant association between the physical body, its centers, and the bodies within it. When this refraction takes place, the ego cannot register its finer intelligence, and the physical body becomes the plaything of its own cell intelligence made more discordant by the spasmodic registrations of the higher mind. It is known only too well that back of all the well-known conditions such as nervous prostration, temporary insanity, nervous disorders, such as psychasthenia, neurasthenia, neuralgia, heart troubles with mental symptoms, morbid forebodings and despondency, mania and goitre, there lurks the abnormal activity of the psychic body, separating the physical body from the natural influx of power.

There are two avenues through which disassociation is brought about. One is through the objective mind by negative, destructive thinking, and the other through the emotions by giving away to negative, inharmonious feelings. Our thoughts are the things which vibrate our physical body, and our emotions are the things which vibrate our psychic bodies, and on the thought will depend the character of the emotion, and an over-intensified psychic feeling will depolarize our flesh. It can be seen that when the association between the psychic self and the physical self has been disturbed, suggestion of the conscious mind to the subconscious is really only a choosing of such a quality of thinking as will reestablish a natural vibratory law between the psychic and physical centers; the link of harmony is conscious, constructive mental activity, which is bound to be followed by harmonious reaction.

When we talk to our sub-self or sub-mind, we are only talking to our objective consciousness, and getting our own physical cell intelligence ready to receive the psychic message, and when we can suspend the action of our own objective mind and send our thoughts and feelings straight into the idea centers of our sub or psychic self, we thus connect the two bodies, and the psychic mind sends the energy back again into our physical cells, and they respond accordingly.

Suggestion to the sub-mind is the simple act of suspending our common thinking altogether, and giving the ego or spirit a chance to speak and to register through our solar plexus on our objective mind and physical body the higher vibratory power. Then when we turn back to common thinking, we find our human mind illumined with a glory not its own and we come after a while to trust our human convictions to the uttermost; for with the touch of our finer states of consciousness, into which we can pass at will, we feel that our own consciousness becomes God-enshrined.

When we know our own physical self and master all its laws, and live in our physical body as a king, we feel that we are conquerors on the physical plane; but when we find our psychic self and master all its laws, and correlate all its power, and pour it through the physical body, adding to this our own natural physical and mental power, then we are greater still, and ready to say, "know!"

When we can suspend or link these two states of consciousness at will, we can pass into the supra-conscious self, and the higher dimensions still waiting for us, and feel the full relationship with our other selves, passing all our attenuated energy through the psychic and physical body, bringing all the energy of the inner selves to bear upon our physical environment, then we are conscious of our power and can speak as one having authority.

In making suggestions to what we called our subconscious mind, we were babes in wisdom, for then we were holding the thought all the time, and trying to make the psychic self do what it already could not choose but do, if we only gave it the chance. In this new understanding we simply let the thought hold us . . we suspend our mixed inharmonious mental currents until they are vibrated into unity with the finer states of consciousness within the self; then we are become not only the holder, but the thing held.

With this knowledge the student no longer spends time with a part of himself which is already finished, but he learns to normally relate himself . . all his atomic consciousness . . with his ego or his own higher constructive mind, and through this ego, and his physical solar center, he has a direct touch with the Universal Mind, and then intelligence pours through all the states of consciousness within him, and his life becomes marked with a new-found power. Is he sick and wants to be healed?

He realizes that disease is nothing but inharmonious vibrations he is registering within his cell sense, and he stops his tense, common mind, and finds another state of consciousness. No one can pass into his higher dimensions of being until he has learned concentration enough to stop thinking when he pleases, and to think of what he pleases for any length of lime. Does he want a new environment?

He realizes again that his environment is made of the same thought-substance as his body, and has the same psychic force and intelligence within it, and that if he will stamp the atoms in space around him with the thought of harmony, sending out from his common thinking mind only vibrations of rhythm, then suspend his thinking and let the finer energy permeate and express through every physical atom, it will not be long until his body and environment will become clothed with atoms corresponding to the higher intelligence under which he is functioning, and with which he has gotten up correspondence.

Man is a complete being, he has evolved through all the kingdom for many, many ages; he has within him derivatives from every plane from which he has evolved; he has latent centers which relate him with those from which he must yet derive. One by one, as he passes through the different dimensions of being, the lower centers of activity atrophy within him from disuse, and, one by one, as he approaches the latent dimension of consciousness which must become expressed, he becomes aware of the awakening of new and unknown powers.

The Secrets, Mysteries & Powers of The Subconscious Mind

As man approaches the time for higher experiences in universal intelligence, he finds the psychic self feebly asserting its existence, and he has new and unrelated experiences in his solar plexus center, and from this faint knowledge men in the past projected the first instruction for its unfoldment, and called it " subconscious mind."

Man is a magnet and he cannot escape feeling and knowing that he is played upon by all magnetic, etheric, radiant and celestial currents of the universe and that they flow through him like the current flows along the line, and he, by giving harmonious response to the play of forces upon him, is unfolded into deeper states of understanding. The subconscious mind and the play of suggestion helped many on their way to fuller harmony, but an understanding of the psychic self and its power, will pass the race into a world of liberty so great that it can become unlimited in its everyday world.

The common mind of man may here and now become illumined through conscious contact with the wider dimensions of consciousness within himself; when he passes into union with this law he transcends the dimensions of the common and subconscious mind and swings out into an orbit of extended power which is only bounded by his own realizations.

Chapter 3

Chapter III

of

Kate Atkinson Boehme's "New Thought Healing Made Plain"

(1918)

The Subconscious Mind

VARIOUS writers use the term "Subconscious" in different ways. With some it describes what I should call instead the Superconscious, or what Emerson called the Over-Soul.

That is not what I mean by the Subconscious, for I use it to denote a product or result of the Conscious. Taken in a large and general sense, the Subconscious might be made to stand for all that is not Conscious, but I consider that it makes the study of Mind and its processes more understandable if we divide it and its functions into Superconscious, Conscious and Subconscious, the Superconscious standing for that vast storehouse from which we draw our thoughts, and of which we know very little, the Conscious standing for what we perceive to be the form of mental activity which we recognize as the human mind, and the Subconscious, standing for automatic mental processes or habits, initiated, in the first instance, by the Conscious Mind.

The Secrets, Mysteries & Powers of The Subconscious Mind

It is of the Subconscious Mind that I will speak in this chapter. To begin with, let us consider its office in controlling the involuntary action of the body, such as the beating of the heart, the circulation of the blood, digestion, etc., any process in fact not immediately set in motion by the will. The act of walking is largely subconscious, but the direction in which one walks is generally dependent on the will, although it often happens that when one goes in the same direction daily the feet will turn certain corners while the Conscious Mind is occupied with other subjects of thought.

The Subconscious Mind is a bundle of habits, and its habits are of long duration. The Subconscious contracts habits of disease; that is, a part of it gets to running irregularly, and keeps on so moving to the disturbance of the general physical harmony, until something happens to set it right, or all the other parts adjust themselves to the erratic action, compromising, as it were, for the sake of temporary peace.

It is well known that the different parts of the body will change position to make room for an organ that is out of place, and though they could perform their work much better in their own proper places, still, after a little grumbling (pain), they settle down to business in their new quarters, and get on quite amicably, though there is always an element of discontent. They do not break out in open riot, but make the owner of the body in which they are ensconced feel somewhat uncomfortable. He knows that something is wrong with the servants in his house, but does not discover what it is.

We have discerned the fact that the physical economy is regulated by intelligence, but have not learned that this regulating intelligence dwells within the organism itself. That it does is one of the strongest points in our healing philosophy.

Long ago, in the early beginnings of life on this planet, that little protoplasmic form, the amoeba, had a natural desire for food. Impelled by this desire, it floated here and there, until it came in contact with the object of its desire, when it folded itself about that object, absorbed from it what it could assimilate, and released the balance. As time went on its desire grew stronger and its need for more varied food greater, so that instead of letting its prey go quickly it held on to it longer, so as to extract from it more sustenance. This resulted finally in a settled, permanent contraction which converted the flat surface of the amoeba into a tube-like formation, the first nucleus of a stomach.

But this stomach could not digest all that it had captured and held, for now it did not give up its prey, and how to get rid of the unused unavailable matter was the question in the amoebic mind. It did not think out the matter as we would do, but set to work to form ducts or channels that served as primitive bowels and kidneys. Later to supply its growing needs it formed the eyes, heart, lungs and other organs.

Note that these organs owe their origin and growth to conscious action on the part of the creature projecting them. No matter how low the form of life, if it has any knowledge of external objects that knowledge may be termed consciousness, for to be conscious means simply to know, the word "conscious" coming from the Latin "conscius," from "con" and "scire," to know. The amoeba was conscious because it knew of the presence of its prey, and it knew enough to grasp that prey. It also had will, for it willed to grasp its prey.

But, as its desires grew apace, it dropped the conscious control of the first established activities, because it could do so by virtue of mechanical law which converts conscious activity into a habit, that becomes automatic, and practically conducts itself without conscious direction or supervision. If you set a ball rolling it is carried forward by the momentum given by your hand, which is the agent of your conscious volition, and the ball rolls on until the force transmitted to it is spent. By the same law the mechanical action set up at first in the body by conscious volition continues until the force imparted to it is exhausted.

In this way our bodies are running on the motive power given to them by conscious volition in the long ago. As we pass from childhood to old age we get farther and farther away from the original impelling force and we finally run down, as in death, just as a clock would that needed winding.

But, just so surely as the clock can renew its action when a new impulse is given it, just so surely can the human body do the same, and in so doing conquer old age and death.

In winding the clock that its action may be renewed you are dealing with a merely mechanical object. In renewing the bodily mechanism you are dealing with living tissues, animated by mind and spirit; therefore, in the latter instance, your tools must be of mind substance because you cannot regulate a thing of mind with a steel tool. You cannot adjust mind substance with a screw driver and hammer. The body is really mind substance, you know, solidified into material atoms and molecules.

Schopenhauer reduced this world to two factors . . Will and Idea. Will stands for the Eternal Energy and Idea for the form it assumes.

I believe this to be true, and as the individual is the Microcosm, or epitome, or microscopic edition of the Macrocosm or Universe, I consider that the motive power of the individual is made up of Will and Idea. Thought is the form that Will resolves itself into; therefore Thought is a Force, and it is the Force with which we adjust and regulate the living tissues of the body.

If you mentally tell a sick person that he is well, no matter how sick he may apparently be, the affirmation falls into his Subconscious Mind, which takes the suggestion and acts upon it, for the Subconscious Mind is sensitive, vibrating mind substance and when it is touched by a living word it moves in accordance with that word.

Living words are words of health, words of success, words of good cheer, and the Subconscious Mind responds to them by setting up better circulation, steadier heart beats, better muscular and nerve action, better sight, better hearing and better digestion.

On the other hand, dead words, such as . . I am sick, miserable, poor, unfortunate and hopeless . . all have a disastrous effect upon the Subconscious Mind, lowering the tone of the whole system and producing the exact opposite of the effect of the live words.

Not once only in the history of the world was the Word made Flesh, but every day, every hour and every moment is it occurring. The Word is continually made Flesh, and happy he who chooses the living Word for his utterance.

If you are told that you are well when you are as sick as you can possibly be and live, it will seem to you like a baseless and false assertion, but it is not, and why?

It is not baseless and false for the reason that your sickness refers to a passing physical state which does not belong to the real you. If I see you in a rage at a certain time, and yet know you to be really a person of equable and sweet temper, shall I pronounce you a savage brute. That is what you seem to be at the moment of observation, but I take into consideration that this passing brain storm does not represent you as I know you to be.

Your bodily sickness is just as much a passing mood of the body, so the New Thought healer takes a firm stand and asserts that you are in reality perfectly well, sound and whole. This is true of the spiritual substance which is really you.

This spiritual you is a Creator. It is an Emanation from the God-Center of all Being and brings with it Divine Power, Creative Power. Its words are living words and are externalized in beautiful, healthy, bodily substance.

Try the effect upon the Subconscious Mind of vigorous, positive, living words. When you are weak affirm that you are strong. Remember the hypnotized subject, who, through suggestion, acquired such tremendous power, though his muscles were flabby and his body puny. The only difference between hypnotic suggestion and autosuggestion is that in the former the conscious mind of the subject is made quiescent, and is thus unable to foist its doubts on the Subconscious Mind, so that the latter, not being handicapped by doubt, can accept the suggestion and act upon it without hindrance. In autosuggestion you will have doubt to contend with, so it will take longer to get results, but if you persist, you will finally cast out doubt and thus obtain a clear channel for Infinite Power to flow through you from center to circumference.

Even though you are overwhelmed by poverty, sickness and sorrow, affirm the opposite. Say with all the earnestness you can muster: I am rich, I am well, I am happy. Say it again and again, day after day, though all things conspire to give the lie to your words. If you do this faithfully you will at last enable the Subconscious Mind to make your words come true.

If you throw bicarbonate of soda into an acid, you correct its acidity. By a law certain and unvarying you can sweeten by affirmation the sourest states of body and environment.

I have proved this in my own life, and knowing what autosuggestion has done for me, I entreat you to see what it will do for you. It calls for persistent effort, but that effort in itself and aside from results is beneficial. You have nothing to lose in the attempt. You risk nothing and you have so much, so very much to gain.

We are too apt to think of the Conscious Mind as the whole of Mind, not understanding that there are mental activities of which we are not aware, but the reasoning, philosophical person accepts on good proof much more in the world than the small part of it that comes under his immediate observation. He believes in suns, stars, planets and worlds that are beyond his cognizance. We have equally good proof of the existence of Mind that is beyond our cognizance. There certainly are mental activities that are carried on without direct volition from the Conscious Mind, and without our knowledge.

When you were a little child, just learning to walk, you had to balance yourself very carefully on one foot while you lifted the other and took a step forward, often losing your balance and falling. After many trials you managed to keep your balance and were then able to walk; but even then you could not run and leap. Those were later efforts. The first attempt to walk led gradually to the later accomplishment. In the meantime the first effort at balance had become a habit, a something automatic that did not call for constant care and attention.

Now you can walk and think about something else all the time. If every day you go to your place of business or to some other destination by the same route, after a while you will not need to think about your course, for you will turn corners unconsciously, and finally arrive at your office or other point, hardly knowing how you reached it. Your walking as mere muscular activity was subconscious, and that which sent your steps in one direction was also subconscious.

Life is made up of these subconscious activities. Without them achievement of a high order would be impossible. At first you learned your letters with difficulty, then words of one syllable, then longer words. Then you learned the various parts of speech . . nouns, verbs, adverbs, adjectives, pronouns, etc. For a long time reading was a matter of slowly spelling out words, but today you grasp whole sentences at a glance. You spell words no longer. All that work is done subconsciously, and with lightning rapidity.

The late Professor James of Harvard, in his "Psychology," stated that art would be impossible were it not for subconscious processes. You can see that this is so, for if the mind had always to busy itself with every detail in art which at first it apprehends with care and precision, there would never be free bold strokes of the brush. All would be cramped and labored like the writing of a child. The free sweep comes from the care given to the earlier detail which falls as a habit into the Subconscious Mind, and is thereafter executed by it.

In my early study of the piano I was an impatient pupil. I could not understand why I was kept on scale and arpeggio, when I thought I could learn to execute them just as well by taking them as they occurred in a piece of music. My music master knew better, and he said, "You must make your technique a habit, so that you can execute runs, etc., unconsciously, for later you will have other things to consider and cannot give your thought at the same time to technique in detail." Some time afterward I saw this to be true, but could not understand it at the moment.

The same rule applies to the study of bettering our physical and mental states. We must hold certain thoughts in the Conscious Mind day after day, possibly month after month, and in some cases even year after year, until they become an essential part of us, until they fall into the Subconscious Mind and set up there an activity.

If you wish to be healthy and carry about with you the magnetic aura of sweetness, goodness and power . . in other words, if you wish to be a radiant success in life, shining with the joy of accomplishment . . you must hold in mind the thoughts that make such attainment possible, and you must go on holding them until they bring results. A fleeting thought will have little or no effect in bringing you the ideal states that you are seeking, but a thought held day after day becomes a tremendous Force in your life. If the thought be true and noble the Subconscious Mind moves to the measure of truth and nobility. If the thought be crafty and mean, the Subconscious moves to that measure. As it moves it registers its processes in the glance of your eye, the turn of your head, the tone of your voice, the movement of your hand, and in many another form of your expression. Your inner self, which you fancy is hidden from observation, is thus constantly revealing itself to others and attracting or repelling their confidence and affection as the case may be, and the confidence and affection of the world around you are two strong factors in winning success. If you are not liked and your life is not a success, look to your inner life and see what is wrong with it. The trouble lies doubtless within yourself instead of in the world outside.

The Subconscious Mind is also creating your physical conditions to the measure of your thought. It does this so silently, so secretly, that you have no idea of its work in affecting the conditions of your body.

You will understand better how you can be unconscious of the activity of the Subconscious, when you notice that you can pursue a long train of thought, and be so absorbed in it that you are not conscious of yourself as thinking, and will not be until you "come to yourself" at the end of your train of thought. Your mind has been working intensely all the while, but you were not conscious of it.

It is certain that the Subconscious Mind pursues a very active course without our cognizance. It is also far-reaching and extends beyond the bounds of our immediate surroundings. It reaches out and works for our good or ill, according to the nature of our thought.

Our best thoughts and purposes come from the Superconscious Mind into the Conscious, and thence proceed into the Subconscious in the form of Habits of Thought. They pass from the immense, illimitable tract of the Superconscious into the comparatively small channel of the Conscious, thence to pass on to that other immense, illimitable tract of the Subconscious, where they become living factors for our weal or woe.

Chapter 4

Chapter I

of

Louis E. Bisch's "Your Inner Self"

(1922)

The Inner Self - The Unconscious or The Subconscious

YOU are what you are today because of everything you have been from the cradle up to the present time.

Thus we summarize the innumerable factors that in their effects combine to produce the character and personality of the human adult. From the moment of birth, nay, even in the mother's womb according to some scientists, every thought, feeling, and experience has a bearing upon mental development. Character and personality are like composites, gradually built up; or better still, like a component of forces constantly changing in an infinite variety of ways with no single factor too insignificant to produce perhaps an indelible impression.

An experience occurring to a child of five may have a direct bearing upon its whole future life. A fright, an unexpected discovery, a love interest during these tender years may be responsible for making or marring an entire career. The shame of undeserved punishment may burn into a child's brain and its scar never be effaced. A dread of closed places ("claustrophobia"), because of which a woman dared not enter an elevator, street car, theatre, or, at times, even her own room, was traceable directly to a shock received at the age of eight when in a game of "hide and seek" a playmate forgot to unlock a closet in which she had been hidden.

Such experiences are often forgotten in fact, usually are. It does not follow that the more important an experience is the more likely it is to be remembered. A factor that determined the failure of a whole lifetime was lost to memory soon after it happened, although its influence was felt indirectly through other channels. The woman mentioned above had completely forgotten the accidental carelessness of her playmate.

This leads to the interesting conclusion that we do not possess simply one mind but, in effect, really two. We have an unconscious or subconscious as well as a conscious mind.

Such a classification may seem arbitrary, and in a sense it is, yet it helps us to understand the curious manifestations of mentality. Like a diamond, the cut surface of which is an inseparable part of the stone mass and the stone mass an inseparable part of its cut surface, so stands the relationship between the conscious and the unconscious. The facets of the diamond have no thickness, they are just the top. Penetrate them for ever so small a fraction of an inch and you immediately have left the surface and are within the stone mass underneath. The latter, in turn, derives its value and brilliancy from the cut surface. One is absolutely and inseparably dependent upon the other.

Consciousness is the medium through which we receive impressions from the outside world. By means of our sense organs eyes, ears, nose, mouth, skin we see, hear, smell, taste, and feel. All these mental images of sight, hearing, smell, taste, and touch linger in consciousness only for the briefest period. Often with astonishing rapidity they are submerged into the underneath, the unconscious, in order to be put away and stored up for future use. The reason consciousness holds them only for a short time is that room must be cleared as quickly as possible for new impressions.

I examined a patient who complained that her thoughts passed to and fro, recurring with maddening repetition. She couldn't thrust ideas away. New impressions thronging from the outside world bewildered her. She no longer could think clearly. Her mind was all in a hodge-podge. In her case consciousness had lost the power of submerging ideas quickly. This woman was developing a mental disease. The conscious mind is the intermediary between the unconscious and the world about us.

We pass a friend in the street; we greet him. We proceed on our way looking at the shop windows, occupied with other thoughts. At night, in conversation at dinner, we recall the meeting of the afternoon and describe it. Having during the interval, for purposes of convenience, stored away the visual image of our friend in the fore-conscious, we are able at will to recall it in minutest detail.

Although the unconscious is actually a storehouse for all our experiences we cannot always lay our hands on them when we want to.

Again, we may have difficulty in banishing a thought, or as we say, forgetting it. This happens when some strong disagreeable emotion is attached to the conscious impression. For example, suppose the man we met has forfeited our friendship by betraying our confidence. Not only shall we have an unpleasant feeling while passing him, but his image and the painful associations it recalls will keep bobbing up again and again into consciousness, and very likely form a continuous undertone to other thoughts, until the pressure is relieved by ventilating the whole incident through the talk at dinner time.

Further, in this underneath mind in this your real inner self there is an orderly arrangement of what is stored away.

Science has already discovered that to certain portions of the brain is given the task of storing up certain kinds of impressions; they have a specialized work to perform. In the back of the head, in the occipital lobes, are the centers for sight. The speech centre is supposed to be on the left side of the brain, above and in front of the ear. Future experimentation will doubtless determine in much greater detail this localization of function. It may be added here that most of the work of the brain seems to be taken up by the left side, the right being, relatively speaking, dormant.

The unconscious has well been called one's historical past. The multitudinous events of each day, but especially its landmarks, are all recorded there.

You will ask whether every experience, important or not, is actually engraved somewhere in the unconscious and is never effaced. Do not some impressions gradually fade out? Is there no such thing as absolute forgetting?

All mental images may conveniently be divided into two types, the purely intellectual and those to which some emotion is attached. The average thinker, pondering the obscurity of Einstein's Law of Relativity, may be exerting the highest intellectual effort of which he is capable, but the subject is so abstract and impersonal that it arouses in him no emotion whatever.

An impression of this intellectual type, when relegated to the unconscious mind, tends to fade out because it lacks the vitalizing element, emotion. To Einstein himself, however, all thought on this great law which he has formulated, is doubtless surcharged with intense emotion.

If, on the other hand, we contemplate even abstractly mother-love, a thrill within us marks the stirring of emotion. If furthermore this thought is transferred from the abstract to the concrete and attached to some woman, the thrill strengthens, the impression made on the unconscious is deepened the record will be permanent.

The mind, in its infinite variety, is indeed a complicated mechanism. Yet it is a machine like any other organ of the body, and its workings can be studied.

The brain is the solid substance or material of that machine. It is made up of various parts called nerve cells and nerve fibers. The functioning or working of these nerve cells produces thoughts. All the thoughts considered together and bound together into a system constitute the mind.

All other organs of the body are machines also and each organ has a definite work to perform. Just as the brain cells manufacture thoughts so do the liver cells manufacture bile and store up sugar in the form of glucose. When all the liver cells are doing their work properly you are pleasantly unaware of their action. When certain of these cells begin to secrete too little and get out of kilter in some way with the rest of the liver, then this organ gets sick and perhaps for the first time you appreciate the fact that you have a liver.

This is the essence of all disease, a disharmony or wrong functioning of the parts of an organ or its disharmony as a whole with the rest of the body. What has been said is true also of the mind. When the mind functions well, when the conscious and the unconscious are working in harmony, there is a sense of well-being, a feeling of being properly and intimately attuned with nature and the world in which we live.

If our two minds are not cooperating, if the inner, unconscious self is in disharmony with the outer, conscious self, well-being disappears and in its stead come uneasiness, worry, and depression.

It is the inner self that we must study, that vast, complicated storehouse that has made us what we are. Let us enter and examine its contents. Perhaps our mental commodities are not labeled correctly, perhaps they have been shelved wrongly or have been mislaid. If we enter fearlessly, ready and willing to face facts as they are without cavil or prejudice, we are certain to profit by the experience if, indeed, we do not actually set our mental houses in order.

Chapter 5

Chapter VIII

of

Henry Thomas Hamblin's "Within You is the Power"

(1920)

The Powers and The Limitations of The Subconscious Mind

THE subconscious mind is the mind of Nature. It possesses extraordinary powers and intelligence, but no inspiration. It is instinctive: it is animal: it is natural: but there is nothing god-like about it . . it is of the earth and the physical plane. It can be described as the inner forces of Nature resident within our body. Having said this we have said nearly all there is to be said about the subconscious, yet this is the mind of which some people have made a veritable god.

The subconscious mind, if led aright, is a very good friend, reducing all repeated thoughts and actions into habit, which, in time, become settled and part of the very life itself. Thus, by conscious right thinking and conscious right action, a good habit is formed, which becomes, in course of time, practically automatic.

This, of course, builds up the character, which, in turn, affects the life. It will be seen, then, how important is the right use of this willing and faithful servant. It is no god, it has no inspiration, but it is a very useful servant, as we shall see.

Most of our actions or movements are done or made subconsciously. The reason that practice makes perfect is that the subconscious mind learns to do the task, and, by so doing, takes it off our hands. How difficult it is to learn to drive a car. How carefully, at first, we have to double declutch and obtain the right engine speed for a noiseless 'change' yet, after a time, the whole action is performed subconsciously. It is the same with piano playing. Many players, some better than others, can play the most difficult classical music without consciously recalling it to mind. As soon as they try to remember the whole 'piece' leaves them, but as long as they leave the whole matter to the subconscious (which never forgets) they can keep on playing. I and my conscious mind are not doing much of the actual writing of this book. We think the thoughts and have something to do with the formation of the sentences, but the subconscious mind writes them down. If I had to think of each word and letter, my task would be hopeless, and I should become half dead with fatigue.

The subconscious mind, however, is even more helpful, for it does the bulk of our thinking, and can be taught to do a great deal more. If we had to think everything out laboriously, according to the laws of logic, life would be unbearable. Instead of this our subconscious mind does the bulk of our thinking, and, if we give it a chance, will do it in an extremely accurate manner, strictly according to the laws of logic and without the slightest fatigue. The more that we train the subconscious to do our ordinary thinking for us, the less we suffer from fatigue. Fatigue is unknown to the subconscious mind, therefore we can never tire it or overwork it.

The Secrets, Mysteries & Powers of The Subconscious Mind

The subconscious mind can be made to do more and more work for us if we will delegate definite work for it to deal with. One who has learnt thought control, who can take up a matter, consider it in all its bearings, and then dismiss the subject from his conscious thought, is able to increase his efficiency a hundred percent, and reduce his mental fatigue almost to vanishing point. Instead of laboriously working out his problems and worrying and scheming over them, he simply dismisses them to his subconscious mind to be dealt with by a master mind which works unceasingly, with great rapidity, extreme accuracy and entirely without effort.

It is necessary, however, to give the subconscious every available information, for it possesses no inspiration or super-human wisdom, but works out logically, according to the facts supplied to it.

This great, natural, untiring 'mind downstairs,' as it has been called, is also capable of doing even more useful work still. A writer or speaker or preacher can collect notes and ideas for his article, book, speech or sermon, and pass them down to his subconscious mind with orders that they be arranged in suitable order, division, subdivision and so on. When he comes either to write or prepare the notes of his speech or sermon, he will find all the work done for him, and all that he has to do is to write it down, entirely without effort or fatigue.

Again, a business man who has learnt to make use of his subconscious mind in this way, need not juggle or worry or fatigue himself by planning and scheming for the future. All that he need do is to submit the facts to the 'greater mind downstairs,' and all the planning will be done for him, entirely without effort, and far more efficiently than he would have done it through laborious conscious thinking.

The Secrets, Mysteries & Powers of The Subconscious Mind

The following, which has just been brought to my notice, is a striking confirmation of the teaching of this chapter:

In a recent issue of Collier's Magazine, an interview with Henry Ford appeared. He spoke of the way with which big business men deal with problems, and pointed out that they did not spend a lot of time pondering and puzzling over plans or ideas. He said: 'An idea comes to us: we think of it for a little while, and then we put it in the pot to boil. We let it simmer for a time, and then take it out.' What Henry Ford means, of course, is precisely what we have been saying, viz., that the idea or problem is dismissed to the subconscious mind, which works it out, and presents it to the conscious mind for judgment.

Yet again, an inventor or one who is constructing something mechanical, can make use of the subconscious mind in precisely the same way. Let him sum up the whole problem, arrange all his facts and available information, and pass them all to the subconscious mind, when, if a successful result is within the range of possibility, an answer or idea will be forthcoming. All this being done, mark you, without any effort whatever.

All this may seem, especially to some readers, rather wonderful and farfetched, yet there is nothing occult or mysterious about it. I am perfectly sure that there is no great writer, politician or business man who does not make use of his subconscious mind in this way. He probably does so unconsciously, but his procedure is the same. Some employ the whole of their mind naturally.

These become men of achievement, who occupy responsible positions, and who bear immense burdens without strain, worry or care. Responsibility sits lightly upon them, and they are serene and untroubled when in positions, and when confronted by tasks and difficulties, such as would drive an ordinary individual out of his mind. Such men develop their powers of attention and concentration (anyone who is in earnest can do this) to a very high degree. They are at great pains to get to the root of a problem, and obtain all the available data possible, but, after that, it is their subconscious mind that does all the work, and which arrives at a decision.

While it comes natural to a few to use their subconscious mind in the correct way, the majority of people find themselves unable to do so. Such, however, can acquire the art by training. First, it is necessary to learn thought control, so as to be able to take up a problem or dismiss it entirely from the mind at will. When a problem is passed on to the subconscious to be worked out, the subject must be dismissed entirely from the conscious mind.

The problem must not be worried over, nor the thoughts allowed to dwell upon it; it must be left entirely to the subconscious. Second, every possible detail and information connected with the problem must be grasped by the conscious mind, and the whole matter, pro and con, visualized before being passed to the subconscious. It will be seen, then, that thought control of a high order is necessary, also powers of attention and concentration. These can all be developed by anyone who is really in earnest.

A good way of starting the use of the subconscious mind is to hold the problem in the mind just as one is going to sleep. There must not, upon any account, be any attempt made to solve the problem or to worry over it. Instead, the main facts of the case, on both sides, must be marshaled, and the case presented to the subconscious mind in much the same way as you would place it before your lawyer.

Having done this, dismiss the whole matter to your subconscious mind, and in most cases you will find in the morning that a solution has been arrived at without any effort or fatigue on your part.

This, of course, is only one of the many ways in which the subconscious mind can, and does, serve its master, or the one who should be master. This great invisible force of Nature is forever working. Whatever ideal is held in the mind becomes woven into the life through the tireless working of the subconscious mind. Only set your attention upon high and lofty achievement, and you will focus all the invisible inward forces of Nature upon its accomplishment.

In course of time you will reap as you sow. If you will direct your attention into the right channel, backing it up with energetic, conscious action, your subconscious will help you day and night, thus making success and achievement possible.

Chapter 6

Chapter XI

of

Eugene Del Mar's "The Conquest of Disease"

(1922)

Conscious and Subconscious

There is a constant struggle for dominance between the conscious and subconscious activities of life; the innate tendency of the conscious being radical and that of the subconscious being conservative. The subconscious is the repository of habits, the nature of which is persistency, and reluctance to change. All sensations find an abiding place in the subconscious fields of activity, which is the realm of emotions, habits, automatism and vital adjustment.

The subconscious represents the ocean of residual mental activities of one's present existence . . if it does not run back of this . . and it dominates his life except to the extent that the conscious faculties challenge or direct it successfully. While always possible to accomplish this purpose often a strong incentive is required.

The subconscious is particularly sensitive to racial ideas and concepts, or to those beliefs and opinions that are being constantly thought, expressed and acted upon by others. In time these are likely to become one's own thought habits, and to constitute the guiding impulses to which constantly one gives ready obedience. It is customary to defer to traditional beliefs and opinions, so that usually one is indisposed to think consciously of these matters except in line with the inclination of the subconscious.

Most people think and speak of traditional beliefs . . particularly of spiritual and religious ones . . in borrowed words, quoting from those who have lived and died long since, and especially from the records of ancient days. Seemingly, these are regarded as having gathered increased authority from age to age, and as possessing a character of sacredness that is lacking in similar statements of the present day. Distance in time seems to lend enchantment to words of wisdom.

We of the Western World worship the beliefs and opinions of our ancestors rather than their persons. On these beliefs and opinions have been established the organizations and institutions of our civilization, and as these constitute or represent the ruling powers of the day, it is deemed by them essential to the well-being of society that these beliefs and opinions remain unchanged. Any challenge to them is considered generally to be dangerous if not intolerable.

There is a universal law of progress that will prevail quite irrespective of what man may do or think concerning it. There is that inner urge of the One Life that cannot be repressed entirely. It may be retarded and delayed, but it will finally break away from a restraint that is too long continued. Inherited traditions and beliefs must have their evolutionary variance and development in correspondence with the necessities of human progress.

Racial thought may be much stimulated and humanity make considerable progress in times of great emotional excitement, such as the years covered by the World War. While this was a period of destruction rather than construction, it witnessed the passing away or the lessened acceptance of some long standing traditional beliefs and opinions that had long outlived their usefulness. To this extent, at least, it answered a useful purpose.

The subconscious is charged with all sorts of negative and destructive beliefs and opinions, and these dominate both one's inner and outer activities unless they are neutralized or overcome by his conscious thought. One's outward activities usually meet with conscious recognition, and therefore one's thoughts that are expressed physically are often changed, altered, corrected or neutralized by conscious thought. But one's erroneous inner activities usually continue unnoticed and unchanged until they evidence themselves in physical discord and disease.

It is essential to health that one counteract the influences on the body of such inherited beliefs and traditional opinions, by conscious activities that will change the subconscious mental attitude from the negative and destructive to the affirmative and constructive. This is the office of the conscious faculties, which have the power and privilege of so impressing the subconscious that it will become subservient to conscious dominion.

In other words, when man does his own thinking, he may dominate his world; but when he permits others to think for him or merely repeats the words of others, he places himself under their direction and control, and offers but slight resistance to the racial thoughts that engulf him. Why remain a parasite when one possesses the divine privilege of thinking for himself?

Before one may change from error to Truth he must know what distinguishes them, and be able to discriminate between the two. He must know how to effect the change, and then do what is necessary to accomplish this purpose. Truth is the invisible essence of the Universe, binding it, correlating it, determining all relations of parts and all sequences of events. It has all of the attributes and qualities of God, the Infinite, Universal Spirit; it is All; it is One, and it is Good. It is ever and always affirmative and constructive; it is eternal, unchanging and universal. All else is error.

The subconscious is surcharged with traditional beliefs and inherited opinions that are based on the misconception of Duality; and that inspire, demand, require or necessitate fear. All of these are false thoughts, productive of mental inharmony and physical disease. They must be transferred from negative and destructive influences to affirmative and constructive ones, if one is to secure mental harmony and physical health. This requires the exercise of the conscious mind, willing to perform the duty of a transforming station; so that the false thought may be changed in character and polarized rightly.

The interpretation of every sensation that suggests fear, discouragement, failure and particularly bodily harm, discord and disease, must be changed from negative to affirmative and from destructive to constructive. With the change thus brought about in subconscious thought, physical conditions are altered accordingly, and both one's inner and outer existence are transformed by the renewing of the mind, through the substitution of constructive elements for destructive ones.

When the subconscious has been trained to disregard false traditional beliefs and inherited opinions, it will substitute constructive thoughts for destructive ones, through the recognition of Principle. Instead of permitting the subconscious to dominate one's life with its inherited and erroneous negative and destructive thoughts, one will charge it with affirmative and constructive thoughts that will assist him to physical health and ease.

One may plant in the subconscious either the dominant note of Principle or of opinion; of Faith and Love or doubt and hate; of health and ease or discord and disease. This dominant note will be the controlling influence in one's life, and it will prevail except where the conscious thought challenges it successfully through definite and intense suggestions to the contrary. Each thought seed will bring forth fruit of its kind, and the dominant thought will be productive of a bounteous crop.

If one impresses upon the subconscious as its dominant note the understanding that God is One, God is All and God is Good; that Principle or Truth is of the essence of all sensation and appearance; that sensation and appearance are therefore always affirmative and constructive, however otherwise they may seem to be; then it becomes comparatively easy for one's conscious thought to impel and direct his life's activities along the path of physical health and ease.

The subconscious never forgets, it never rests, it is eternally persistent; while the conscious is neglectful, intermittent and spasmodic. The subconscious is always awake, even while the conscious sleeps. These qualities and attributes of the subconscious are of tremendous import and advantage to one when its dominant note represents the knowledge of Principle, and is therefore affirmative and constructive.

The conversion of the subconscious from a negative and destructive quality to one of affirmative and constructive influence is brought about by conscious thought, speech and action of the latter character. The more clear, definite, forceful and intense the conscious activities, the deeper is the impression that will be made on the subconscious. One should feel what he thinks and affirms. The more definite the challenge and the greater the conviction behind the conscious thought and activities, the more effectually will the subconscious inheritances and acquired habits of false thinking be overcome and changed.

Behind the affirmation of Truth is the thought of it, and the power of the affirmation depends upon the conviction, or the Faith and Love that it represents. Idle and indifferent affirmations are of but slight importance; automatic duplication of words is lifeless and impotent; the spoken word has power in the Truth that it symbolizes and the realization that vitalizes it. The most effective affirmations are those that are vitalized, through being lived, expressed and manifested in one's physical activities.

Before the conscious faculties were given creative power over the expressions of the One Life, the subconscious was in sole control. It is essential that it retains this control, except to the extent that the conscious faculties assume the responsibility of direction and cooperation. When the conscious mind accepts this leadership in the knowledge of Truth, the subconscious becomes its faithful ally in the cause of mental harmony and physical health.

The conscious impresses its will by means of suggestions, which the subconscious receives and then obeys. In its obedience, it contracts habits that become increasingly difficult to change as time goes on, and especially if these habits are in accord with and sustained by racial habits of thought. The subconscious becomes increasingly reluctant to believe that it is the will of the conscious to change or alter its time-honored instructions. In its loyalty to these, it requires positive evidence of the change in conscious desire, and it is justified in demanding convincing proof in the way of clear, definite and positive command.

One's purpose should be the harmonious activity of the conscious and subconscious on the plane of affirmative and constructive thought, so that one's physical activities will receive the stimulus of not only the intellectual conviction but also the emotional qualities of Faith and Love. As man is primarily emotional, it is seldom that his reason dominates when his emotions run counter to it. The subconscious ocean is likely to overwhelm his conscious stream of thought; but their cooperation will add to the power of the conscious stream the full force of the ocean of the subconscious.

It does not necessarily require as long a time to overcome a thought habit as it took to acquire it. It depends upon the intensity of one's desire, the depth of one's previous false convictions, and the completeness of one's realization of Truth. The habits of a lifetime may be overcome in an instant. One may have trod the path of error all of his life, and yet have the ability to right-about-face in a moment. One need but seek Truth and he shall find it if his search for it be earnest and sincere. One has but to turn away from the darkness of falsity to be flooded with the light of Truth.

Chapter 7

Elsie Lincoln Benedict's "How to Unlock Your Subconscious Mind Through the Science of Mental Analysis"

(1922)

Your Secret, Subconscious Self

FROM the deck of a steamer you see an iceberg. Always afterward you think of it as consisting of just what you saw no more and no less. You describe its outlines to your friends and explain its size and shape as being what was visible to your eye.

Yet you saw but one-tenth of that iceberg. The other nine-tenths were floating beneath the surface, entirely out of sight.

If you have never seen a big iceberg, drop a miniature one into your glass next time you are at table, and the same thing on a smaller scale will happen.

Your mind is like that iceberg. It has its upper and nether parts .. the conscious and subconscious. The conscious may be likened to the tenth of the iceberg which is discernible above the surface, for its operations and processes are always apparent to you. It consists of the thoughts you think from moment to moment in your waking hours, but lose when you fall asleep.

This conscious mind is busy handling the experiences which arise in your environment .. the "awareness" of your surroundings, sensations of what you are doing, seeing, tasting, touching, smelling. All plans, visualizations and imaginings which catch and hold your attention are also a part of this surface mind.

You express this conscious mind more or less externally and can readily detect its operations. You can open the door on it any instant and catch it at work. Right now, for instance, you can watch your mind thinking of this page and what you are reading. You can look on while it reasons, judges and decides about what is printed here.

In short, this conscious element of your mind is the mind we are all familiar with, the mind we have always known we possessed, the mind dealt with in academic psychology, the mind that does our conscious thinking.

The Submerged Nine-Tenths

But recent discoveries have shown that this surface mind, which we had supposed comprised all our mental processes, is less than one-tenth of the total human consciousness.

These discoveries reveal that underneath this conscious mind, part and parcel of it, bound up and wound around it, powerfully influencing it but out of sight are the "submerged nine-tenths" called the subconscious.

What Is The Subconscious?

This subconscious is the warehouse in which you have been unconsciously and involuntarily storing away all the impressions, memories, feelings, accumulated force and "aftermaths" of everything that has ever happened to you.

The Secrets, Mysteries & Powers of The Subconscious Mind

This means not only all the things you are conscious of having experienced but millions of sensations you were unaware of at the time. All have stowed themselves away down there in the pigeonhole of that submerged nine-tenths of your consciousness, to be heard from later in life.

Many of the mysteries about yourself which have baffled, discouraged or inspired you are solved by the new science of Mental Analysis, which explains this secret self that lies deeply buried but always active within each of us.

Retail and Wholesale Thinking

The conscious mind may be called the "retailer mind." It is compelled to deal with non-essentials, the externals of your hourly experiences, the thousands of details that arise in your immediate environment. But your subconscious mind knows nothing of these. All its power is directed toward the attainment of your deepest desires. It is a wholesaler and does things only in the by-and-large.

It is not so much concerned with what you are doing, saying or experiencing at this moment, as with the massed result of the experiences through which you have already passed, plus the probable effect upon you of those you are now facing.

Your subconscious mind does not so much think as feel. It does not believe or reason, as does your conscious mind. It knows.

Your Subconscious Ocean

Nothing you see, hear, say, think, do, feel, or experience is ever lost. Each is preserved forever in the deeps of your subconsciousness.

It is as though you lived in a houseboat on a great ocean, into whose depths something dropped every time you had a thought, a feeling or any kind of experience whatever.

Some of these are of such a nature as to throw overboard the seeds from which would grow beautiful water lilies, ferns and lacey mosses. Some would bring forth weeds, others poison ivy, while others would fringe the shore with great trees whose strength would delight you and whose shade would comfort and bless all who came that way.

Some of your deeds and desires would fling into this ocean only trash . . chunks of pig iron, bits of wood, baubles, toys, debris . . trappings and trimmings of idle moments, dark thoughts, primitive instincts . . all would lie there at the bottom of the sea. Divers could find every one . . some distorted, some washed cleaner than when they went in, but each and every one affected in some way by being there.

Many of the thoughts and things we had supposed lifeless would turn out to be fertile seeds. They would have sprouted all manner of strange, exotic, ugly and beautiful plants, each bearing fruit according to its nature and sending up to the ocean's surface the results natural to itself.

We do and say many things which are the result of the things we previously submerged in this subconscious sea.

The Stranger in Your Skin

A man does things that are "foreign" to him . . not what he intended. They seem to do themselves.

He means to say a certain thing, to express a certain thought and instead says something entirely different. He forgets the names of people he knows perfectly well, answers

"No" when he means "Yes," and in a hundred ways entangles himself against his will.

He says "that was accidental," "I said that unconsciously" or "I wasn't myself." But none of these is really true. The fact of the matter is that all of them were done by his subconscious. They are not accidental but in accordance with the definite law that we tend constantly to express to the outer world whatever is in the back of our minds.

We also tend to forget whatever is displeasing to the ego and to remember whatever is pleasing to it.

The Actor's Story

One of the well known actors in America told us this:

"I am often asked to dinners and other social affairs with people in whom I have no interest whatever . . people with whom I have nothing in common and with whom I would rather not be bothered.

"I found that almost invariably I jotted down these engagements on my calendar for the day following the actual date, and was always being called up afterward and reminded of my absence.

"After a while it dawned on me that my subconscious wish not to go caused me habitually but innocently to put down the wrong date and always to make the mistake for the day after so that it would be safely over before I could be reminded.

"I arrived at these conclusions because of another strange experience I was always having of putting down engagements with personal friends for the date previous to that in the invitation, evidently because I was subconsciously anxious to go.

"More than once I arrived at these houses a day or even two days prior to the party as unconscious of this mistake as I was of the opposite one"

In Our Own Lives

In a lesser degree these experiences happen to all of us . . as when we find it so easy to be early at any affair we wish to attend, but late to things we dislike.

Memory's Treasure Vault

The subconscious has also been called "the treasure vault of memory." In it is preserved the record of everything we have ever heard, seen, read, learned.

It never forgets. Everything you ever knew you know still . . whether your memory is able to dive down and bring it from the bottom of your consciousness at this moment or not.

One reason why all persons are not able to, do this now is that we have, until the last few years, been ignorant of the fact that the mind did remember, and have taken it for granted that things passed entirely out of our mental grasp . . that we had "forgotten."

A clearer understanding of the subconscious enables even the beginner to revive in consciousness many things he had imagined completely erased from memory.

The Subconscious Never Sleeps

The subconscious is always on the alert. We now know with complete certainty that it never sleeps .. in fact, that it is more active when the conscious mind sleeps than during our waking hours.

We have seen proof of this many times in our own lives .. as, for instance, when we can awaken without an alarm clock to catch a 4 a. m. train if we really want to take the journey.

Nurses in hospital wards full of patients sleep soundly through all manner of outcries but awaken at the whispered request of their own patients. A mother sleeps through many disturbances but rouses at the merest movement of her sick child.

The country man upon coming to the city is unable to sleep the first few nights but his subconscious soon adapts itself and he sleeps as soundly through those same noises a week later as he did out on the farm.

Bridge Between Mind and Body

"Does the mind have a body or does the body have a mind?" is a question over which the philosophers have wrangled for centuries. Today we know that both are true and that the subconscious mind, of which these ancient arguers were unaware, is the bridge between the body and the mind.

The conscious mind functions through the brain but the subconscious functions throughout the entire body .. the cerebrum, the muscles, the solar plexus, the nerves apparently through every cell in both body and brain.

That this is no far-fetched theory is shown in the fact that its first American exponent was that greatest living material scientist, Thomas A. Edison. He says, "Every cell in us thinks" and has proven to his own satisfaction that nothing is dead matter but all is living energy expressing itself in various forms.

Inner Recesses and Outer Results

There have always been those who realized the influence of these submerged selves of ours and there is not a thinking human but who realizes that many things in his life, however much they may mystify others, are but the outward expression of something in his inner life.

But it requires an unusually high grade of intelligence and an unusually frank heart to acknowledge what Mental Analysis shows us so clearly today . . that:

Your money,
Your possessions,
Your good luck and bad luck,
Your ill health or perfect health,
Your environment,
Your life as a whole

are the harvests from seeds you planted in the soil of your subconscious in days gone by.

But whether you realize it or not, these things are true. You are reaping what you have sown. The results are in accordance with laws . . laws that are inexorable, unchanging, and absolutely impersonal.

The Secrets, Mysteries & Powers of The Subconscious Mind

Your life today is the net result of your yesterdays. Your tomorrows will be the net result of those yesterdays plus the seeds you are planting today, this hour and this instant.

The only way to make the tomorrows what you wish them to be is to learn what you have already planted, how to uproot the weak and cultivate the strong things that are growing in your personality, and how to plant from this hour onward only the seeds whose fruit you desire to reap in your coming years.

This course, by showing you these things, can enable you to remake your life, as it has already done for thousands of our former students.

The Secret of the Famous

All great souls have recognized and declared that they were strangely aided by something within themselves but which they did not "reason out."

Every famous composer has said, "No, I can't tell you how I thought out the music because I did not do so. It came to me. I put down what came."

Every great poet has said, "I cannot tell you how I wrote this poem because I do not know. It said itself in my mind, and I wrote it down".

Every famous orator has said, "The right thoughts never come when I am trying to write out a speech. My audience is the other half of me. The best ideas come only when I am face to face with the crowd."

Every illustrious minister has declared, "The best parts of my sermons are never written in my study but come into my mind as I stand before my congregation."

The flash of inspiration" which comes to the lawyer at the crucial moment in his trial of a case, comes not from his conscious but from his subconscious mind, as he will tell you himself.

The reason so few people achieve greatness is not that there are but few with the spark of genius in them, but the source of greatness . . the subconscious mind . . is clogged in all but the few. The mental machinery of most people is full of monkey wrenches and junk, the brakes are all on and the cylinders are skipping.

The average mind is as disorganized as a rag bag.

Dr. Jekyll and Mr. Hyde

Almost every individual leads a Dr. Jekyll and Mr. Hyde life, with part of his mind pulling one way and another pulling the opposite. Then he wonders why this split personality makes no more progress.

There is no mystery about it. Such a man is never able to present a solid front to the world.

A unified personality is the first requisite for success or happiness under any condition whatever.

The energies, mentality and interests of the average individual are disorganized, disrupted, chaotic, jumbled in a mixed-up heap. Few people see the ruinous effect of this splitting of the personality, and some even consider it an achievement.

A man calls himself clever when he is able to live one life outwardly and another inwardly. He is able to appear at a social affair disliking the whole thing . . the guests, the interruption to his business, even the hostess . . and all the while talk and act as though charmed, flattered, delighted and happy.

"Society compels me to lead this double life," he will say, "My business requires it, social amenities demand it." Good gracious, what an insufferable bore!" he exclaims to his wife the instant they are out of earshot.

And to an extent these are true. But we are coming to realize that insincerity of any kind, reacts back on the personality with fatal consequences.

First among these consequences is the disintegrating of the consciousness and no man can succeed whose two minds are not working in harmony.

The Penalty of Pretense

It is not easy to lead double lives, even though they be comparatively innocent ones. Concealed facts are always popping out into open sight. Slips of the tongue, glances and postures . . a hundred things betray the man who would keep out of sight his real and actual self.

The subconscious is like a vast irrigation system with every muscle a tiny headgate in the great network. A man may learn to watch one or two or even a dozen of these headgates in eyes, mouth, voice and manner . . but they are so numerous he cannot watch them all, and from whence he least expects it there will break out the tell-tale overflow.

A Practical Personal Science

This latest of the human sciences shows us what we have been doing to ourselves, our lives, our chances in life, our loves, hopes and aspirations; how we have been unconsciously poisoning our own wells at their source; how we have administered mental narcotics to ourselves when we most needed mental stimulation; how we have built up the present from our own individual, racial and biological past into a structure in which we now live and through which our personalities function, express themselves and meet the world.

It shows how we may easily and immediately reverse the process and begin to get the things we want out of life.

It is an essentially practical, personal science, dealing with our everyday problems in an everyday way.

Our aim and our accomplishment to date has been to give it to the student in such simple and straightforward language that it begins from the first moment to help him in the solution of his most intimate, inward affairs. It will do this for you. It will give you the insight into your own mentality which will explain to you —

Why you think and feel as you do;
Why you have gotten no farther in life;
Why some succeed and others fail.

What Are You Preparing For?

Elbert Hubbard stated a great truth when he said, "We get what we prepare for."

People bring their own unhappiness. That they do so innocently, blindly, unknowingly does not help matters. "Ignorance of the law excuses no man."

The laws which rule us and our lives are divine, unalterable. He who obeys them, whether he do so consciously or unconsciously, reaps the rewards that other people call "good luck." He who consciously or unconsciously violates them pays the penalties he calls his "bad luck."

The supremest effort of life, therefore, should be to learn what the laws are which rule human happiness and how they operate, that we may consciously and constantly plant the seeds for the harvests we want.

This course in Mental Analysis has made these laws so clear, concise, graphic and understandable that anyone can put them to use in the solving of his everyday problems. They bring results from the first moment of applying them, in happiness, health and success.

Skepticism and Criticism

Some may say, "These things sound impossible" It is inevitable that some would say this. Every step in human progress has been opposed at first and forced to fight its way to recognition against skepticism and criticism.

This is due to the well-known psychological fact that the average individual does not think for himself, even about his own most serious problems, but gives himself ready-made and outworn excuses for his failures and flatteringly false congratulations for his success.

Such a one refuses to believe a new thing because it is new. Thinking men and women know that the human race is in the infant stage of its development; that a few hundred years from now human beings will be doing things as far beyond our present achievements as ours are beyond those of prehistoric man.

And those who have given the subject thought realize that this progress is coming, as it has already begun to come, through the one thing that has given man sovereignty over the globe . . further understanding and development of his consciousness.

Man is superior to animals in proportion as his mind is superior to theirs. One man is superior to another and achieves results superior to the other's in exact proportion as his mind is in better working order, more under his control and better understood by him.

Why We Were Not Told

"If I bring my own sufferings and successes why have I not been taught this before?" others will ask.

There is but one answer. We are never taught the things most vital to human happiness.

Fathers and mothers are so busy getting food for their children's stomachs and clothes for their backs, they have no time or energy to investigate or explain either to themselves or to their children how the human mind controls human happiness.

The result is that parents who would not think of feeding their children's intestines canned food, feed their intellects with canned ideas . . ideas so outworn, so stale and putrid that the child is forever handicapped in the race of life.

Teachers and preachers . . the other two forces which train the young mind . . are so harassed by the overpowering problem of making small salaries suffice for necessities that they have neither heart nor head for remoter human ones.

Favorite Fibs

Thus we grow up, knowing "a lot of things that ain't so" . . things that are easy to teach, pretty to preach, but impossible to live up to.

We are told that "virtue is its own reward" . . and see the most virtuous people all around us rewarded with kicks and poverty.

We are told that "genius is the art of taking infinite pains" . . only to discover that the most painstaking people are in bookkeeping cages getting $20 a week, while every genius is notoriously incapable of taking pains with anything save what he loves . . even his shoe laces!

We are taught that "success comes from hard work" . . but note how the day laborer gets four dollars for working his hands eight hours, while the banker makes a fortune by working his head four hours a day and playing golf the rest of the time.

The Secret of Success

The secret of success is not hard work, painstaking effort, nor even virtue . . though each of these is essential to supreme happiness The secret of success for every human being lies in the harmonious working of his conscious and subconscious powers.

Those who have succeeded have, in every instance, consciously or unconsciously, used their minds as they were intended to be used; those who failed unconsciously violated the laws of the mind and reaped the inevitable result.

Purpose of the Subconscious

This submerged nine-tenths of the consciousness is of the utmost significance in every human life. It has unlimited capacity for good or evil, according as it is used or misused. Each individual's life is made or marred by this vast subterranean sea of urges and impulses.

This great self is infinitely strong, infinitely courageous, infinitely powerful. It exists for one purpose, and one only . . to externalize you, to bring you self-expression, to secure for you an untrammeled personality, to attain for you your supreme subconscious aim.

From birth to death it strives to set you free, to enable you to be yourself, your truest, realest self; that happy successful self you were created to be; the great self you may be, can be, and shall be.

The Supreme Wish

The greatest psychological discovery of recent ages shows us that the entire personality of every human being is built around someone deep, consuming desire . . some supreme subconscious wish.

In one individual this supreme desire is for one thing, in another for something else, depending on the type and temperament of each, but no human being lives who does not have some deep desire at the core of his heart.

Life Built Around the Wish

That every man builds his life around this supreme wish is the explanation of many of our otherwise incredible inconsistencies, strange reactions, and of the remarkable accomplishments of apparently mediocre men and women.

Many persons know what their supreme life wish is. The most successful always know, and their success is due more to this knowledge than to any other one thing.

When we say "that man knows his own mind," we are saying much more than we realize. For there are many who do not know and these many are the failures in life.

Those who only guess are the half-failures.

No Hard Work Necessary

In utilizing your subconsciousness, strenuous effort is neither necessary nor desirable.

This mind is already organized and ready to work out for you whatever you desire. It does not need urging. It is the real you. It contains all your aspirations and impulses already. It does not require encouragement any more than a river needs to be encouraged to flow to the sea.

All it needs is direction. It is keyed for action, and has been every day since you were born. It is like a race horse that has been trained for the track. Take the reins in your hand and let it work for you.

You have never tested the powers within your own personality because society, schools, teachers, preachers and parents are organized against every kind of spontaneous expression of the individual.

That is why it is in danger of committing suicide . . this society of ours. That is why some of its members are constantly turning against it and doing damage in the form of murder and war.

We must live understanding^ before we can live uprightly.

"Getting Out of Yourself"

Do not waste time and energy trying to "get out of yourself." The man who tries to get out of himself before he has cleaned house is working in the wrong direction.

The person who feels impelled to get out of himself has something wrong inside which he cannot bear to look at. So he goes to the theatre, drinks, gambles, speeds, scolds, spends money and time foolishly.

But it does no good. He cannot get away from himself. The moment the excitement is over back he slumps to the old self which is worse than it was before, because it knows and he knows the wasting of time, energy, money and thought in the attempt to drown his troubles has harmed him, entangled him more deeply and pushed him farther back than ever.

The teaching, "forget yourself for the world " is a beautiful ideal . . one we must more and more live up to if we hope to be truly happy. It is necessary to the progress of the world for us to lose ourselves in self-forgetful service.

But we must learn how to do it. No one takes very long steps toward it until he settles his "internal warfare."

Every Day Illustrations

Your subconscious is either backing your work or "bucking it." It will back you in anything that is in accordance with your supreme wish. You will do the amazing tasks with amazing ease once you start.

But anything which is in opposition to it will go slowly, sadly, heavily, and inefficiently Whatever aids and abets your supreme subconscious aim you will labor over for long hours absolutely without fatigue, but whatever takes you in the opposite direction leaves you actually physically exhausted at the end of ten minutes.

How gladly and gaily we do a task today when it furthers some particular project! How glumly and grumpily we do the very same thing tomorrow if it no longer furthers that project.

With what vim a young girl who has always disliked housework helps mother with dinner and the dishes when her young man is there to see!

How easy it is to forget the bills we owe . . but how that same memory of ours does work when the other fellow owes us!

How simple to remember the addresses, the initials, and even the telephone numbers of new people we are interested in, and how difficult to remember even the names of those we are indifferent to! The only difference in all these cases is the difference in the way in which a subconscious wish is affected.

"If it is possible for my subconscious to get for me anything I wish why have I never gotten the things I most desired?" is a reasonable and inevitable question. Because you have violated the laws whereby the subconscious operates.

You, like everything else in the universe, are a part OF, not apart FROM natural law. Your being is responsive to and built in accordance with certain divine rules, regulations and edicts. When you disobey those you suffer, when you obey them you succeed.

The First Law of the Subconscious

You must free your subconscious of the shackles with which you have all your life crippled it; you must take off the throttles with which you have been choking it; you must give the strong self of you a chance to work for you; you must take your hands off the bridle of this swift racer that champs at the bit, and let him go.

Every great, successful, big or famous person has differed from the failures wholly and solely in proportion as he learned there was a deep voice within him, listened to that voice, and let it out for all the world to hear!

Your Problem Is You

First of all get rid of the notion that people and things and life in general are "against you." Nothing can harm you but yourself and the only way you can permanently hurt yourself is by the misuse of your mentality.

Luck is not against you. Luck is what you make it. Conditions and circumstances may be adverse to you at this moment, but if so, they are the ones you have made by your previous thinking. Stop that kind of thinking or you will go on piling up more adverse conditions for tomorrow.

Your Invisible Self

Your subconscious may be compared to a great ocean liner. As we gaze at her across the blue ocean what do we see?

The Secrets, Mysteries & Powers of The Subconscious Mind

We say we see the steamer. But what we see is her upper decks, masts and fluttering flags; the waving, smiling passengers . . the life and action of her.

But there is far more to that steamer than this. There is her great body . . the lower regions, the steerage, the hundreds of workmen, tons of cargo, massive machinery and powerful dynamos.

The upper decks look important, but the thing that determines how far and how fast she travels, what she carries, and whether or not she ever reaches port, depend on the way the unseen forces work down there in her hull.

The outside of you that men see are your upper decks. People, and perhaps you yourself, imagine these are all there is to you.

But it is only a fraction. The direction in which you go, what you do with your life, how far you travel and the port at which you arrive, all depend on the workings of the subconscious mind down there in your hull.

That subconscious is not only nine-tenths of your mind but nine-tenths of you. It is far stronger than anything and everything else within you, utterly fearless and unafraid.

It possesses powers beyond your wildest dreams. When you put yourself in harmony with it, it will carry you surely and safely to your desired destination.

Chapter 8

Chapter IV

of

Christian Larson's "Your Forces And How To Use Them"

(1912)

The Forces of The Subconscious

WHEN you think of yourself do not think of that part of yourself that appears on the surface. That part is the smaller part and the lesser should not be pictured in mind. Think of your larger self, the immense subconscious self that is limitless both in power and in possibility. Believe in yourself but not simply in a part of yourself. Give constant recognition to all that is in you, and, in that all have full faith and confidence.

Give the bigger being on the inside full right of way. Believe thoroughly in your greater interior self. Know that you have something within you that is greater than any obstacle, circumstance or difficulty that you can possibly meet. Then in the full faith in this greater something, proceed with your work.

In using the power of the mind, the deeper the action of thought, will and desire, the greater the result. Accordingly, all mental action to be strong and effective, must be subconscious; that is, it must act in the field of the mental undercurrent as it is in this field that things are actually done. Those forces that play upon the surface of mind may be changed and turned from their course by almost any outside influence, and their purpose thus averted. But this is never true of the undercurrents. Anything that gets into the mental undercurrents will be seen through to a finish, regardless of external circumstances or conditions; and it is with difficulty that the course of these currents is changed when once they have been placed in full positive action.

It is highly important therefore that we permit nothing to take action in these undercurrents that we do not wish to encourage and promote; and for the same reason, it is equally important that we cause everything to take action in these currents that we do wish to encourage and promote. These undercurrents, however, act only through the subconscious, and are controlled by the subconscious. In consequence, it is the subconscious which we must understand and act upon if we want the power of mind to work with full capacity and produce the greatest measure possible of the results desired.

In defining the subconscious mind, it is first necessary to state that it is not a separate mind. There are not two minds. There is only one mind in man, but it has two phases . . the conscious and the subconscious. We may define the conscious as the upper side of the mentality, and the subconscious as the underside. The subconscious may also be defined as a vast mental field permeating the entire objective personality, thereby filling every atom of the personality through and through.

We shall come nearer the truth, however, if we think of the subconscious as a finer mental force, having distinct powers, functions and possibilities, or as a great mental sea of life, energy and power, the force and capacity of which has never been measured. The conscious mind is on the surface, and therefore we act through the conscious mind whenever mental action moves through the surface of thought, will or desire, but whenever we enter into deeper mental action and sound the vast depths of this underlying mental life, we touch the subconscious, though we must remember that we do not become oblivious to the conscious every time we touch the subconscious, as the two are inseparably united.

That the two phases of the mind are related can be well illustrated by comparing the conscious mind with a sponge, and the subconscious with the water permeating the sponge. We know that every fiber of the sponge is in touch with the water, and in the same manner, every part of the conscious mind, as well as every atom in the personality, is in touch with the subconscious, and completely filled, through and through, with the life and the force of the subconscious.

It has frequently been stated that the subconscious mind occupies the Fourth. Dimension of space, and though this is a matter that cannot be exactly demonstrated, nevertheless, the more we study the nature of the subconscious, as well as the Fourth Dimension, the more convinced we become that the former occupies the field of the latter. This, however, is simply a matter that holds interest in philosophical investigation. Whether the subconscious occupies the Fourth Dimension or some other dimension of space will make no difference as to its practical value.

In order to understand the subconscious, it is well at the outset to familiarize ourselves with its natural functions, as this will convince ourselves of the fact that we are not dealing with something that is beyond normal mental action.

The subconscious mind controls all the natural functions of the body, such as the circulation, respiration, digestion, assimilation, physical repair, etc. It also controls all the involuntary actions of the body, and all those actions of mind and body that continue their natural movements without direction from the will. The subconscious perpetuates characteristics, traits, and qualities that are peculiar to individuals, species and races. What is called heredity therefore is altogether a subconscious process. The same is true of what is called second nature.

Whenever anything has been repeated a sufficient number of times to have become habitual, it becomes second nature, or rather a subconscious action. It frequently happens, however, that a conscious action may become a subconscious action without repetition, and thus becomes second nature almost at once.

When we examine the nature of the subconscious, we find that it responds to almost anything the conscious mind may desire or direct, though it is usually necessary for the conscious mind to express its desire upon the subconscious for some time before the desired response is secured. The subconscious is a most willing servant, and is so competent that thus far we have failed to find a single thing along mental lines that it will not or cannot do. It submits readily to almost any kind of training, and will do practically anything that it is directed to do, whether the thing is to our advantage or not.

In this connection, it is interesting to learn that there are a number of things in the human system usually looked upon as natural, and inevitable, that are simply the results of misdirected subconscious training in the past. We frequently speak of human weaknesses as natural, but weakness is never natural. Although it may appear, it is invariably the result of imperfect subconscious training. It is never natural to go wrong, but it is natural to go right, and the reason why is simple.

Every right action is in harmony with natural law, while every wrong action is a violation of natural law. It has also been stated that the aging process is natural, but modern science has demonstrated that it is not natural for a person to age at sixty, seventy, or eighty years. The fact that the average person does manifest nearly all the conditions of old age at those periods of time, or earlier, simply proves that the subconscious mind has been trained through many generations to produce old age at sixty, seventy, eighty or ninety, as the case may be, and the subconscious always does what it has been trained to do.

It can just as readily be trained, however, to produce greater physical strength and greater mental capacity at ninety than we possess at thirty or forty. It can also be trained to possess the same virile youth at one hundred as the healthiest man or woman of twenty may possess. In fact, practically every condition that appears in the mind, the character and the personality of the human race, is the result of what the subconscious mind has been directed to do during past generations.

It is therefore evident that as the subconscious is directed to produce different conditions in mind, character, and personality . . conditions that are in perfect harmony with the natural law of human development, such conditions will invariably appear in the race. Thus we understand how a new race or a superior race may appear upon this planet.

There are a great many people who are disturbed over the fact that they have inherited certain characteristics or ailments from their parents, but what they have inherited is simply subconscious tendencies in that direction, and those tendencies can be changed absolutely. What we inherit from our parents can be eliminated so completely that no one would ever know it had been there. In like manner, we can improve so decidedly upon the good qualities that we have inherited from our parents that any similarity between parent and child in those respects would disappear completely.

The subconscious mind is always ready, willing and competent to make any change for the better in our physical or mental make-up that we may desire, though it does not work in some miraculous manner, nor does it usually produce results instantaneously. In most instances its actions are gradual, but they invariably produce the results intended if the proper training continues.

The subconscious mind will respond to the directions of the conscious mind so long as those directions do not interfere with the absolute laws of nature. The subconscious never moves against natural law, but it has the power to so use natural law that improvement along any line can be secured. It will reproduce in mind and body any condition that is thoroughly impressed and deeply felt by the conscious mind. It will bring forth undesirable conditions when directed to produce such conditions, and it will bring forth health, strength, youth and added power when so directed.

If you continue to desire a strong physical body, and fully expect the subconscious to build for you a stronger body, you will find that this will gradually or finally be done. You will steadily grow in physical strength. If you continue to desire greater ability along a certain line and expect the subconscious to produce greater mental power along that line, your ability will increase as expected, but it is necessary in this connection to be persistent and persevering.

To become enthusiastic about these things for a few days is not sufficient. It is when we apply these laws persistently for weeks, months and years that we find the results to be, not only what we expected, but frequently far greater. Everything has a tendency to grow in the subconscious. Whenever an impression or desire is placed in the subconscious, it has a tendency to become larger and therefore the bad becomes worse when it enters the subconscious, while the good becomes better. We have the power, however, to exclude the bad from the subconscious and cause only the good to enter that immense field.

Whenever you say that you are tired and permit that feeling to sink into the subconscious, you will almost at once feel more tired. Whenever you feel sick and permit that feeling to enter the subconscious, you always feel worse. The same is true when you are weak, sad, disappointed or depressed. If you let those feelings sink into your subconscious, they will become worse.

On the other hand, when we feel happy, strong, persistent and determined, and permit those feelings to enter the subconscious, we always feel better. It is therefore highly important that we positively refuse to give in to any undesirable feeling. Whenever we give in to any feeling, it becomes subconscious, and if that feeling is bad, it becomes worse; but so long as we keep undesirable feelings on the outside, so to speak, we will hold them at bay, until nature can readjust itself or gather reserve force and thus put them out of the way altogether.

We should never give in to sickness, though that does not mean that we should continue to work as hard as usual when not feeling well, or cause mind and body to continue in their usual activities. When we find it necessary, we should give ourselves a complete rest, but we should never give in to the feeling of sickness. The rest that may be taken will help the body to recuperate, and when it does the threatening ailment will disappear. When you feel tired or depressed, do not admit it, but turn your attention at once upon something that is extremely interesting . . something that will completely turn your mind towards the pleasing, the more desirable or the ideal. Persist in feeling the way you want to feel, and permit only wholesome feelings to enter the subconscious.

Thus wholesome feelings will live and grow, and after awhile your power to feel good at all times will have become so strong that you can put out of the way any adverse feeling that may threaten at any time. In this connection, we may mention something that holds more than usual interest. It has been stated by those who are in a position to know, that no one dies until they give up; that is, gives in to those adverse conditions that are at work in their system, tending to produce physical death.

So long as he or she refuses to give in to those conditions, they continue to live. How long a person could refuse to give in even under the most adverse circumstances is a question, but one thing is certain, that thousands and thousands of deaths could be prevented every year if the patient in each case refused to give in. In many instances, the forces of life and death are almost equally balanced. Which one is going to win depends upon the mental attitude of the patient. If he or she gives over the mind and will to the side of the forces of life, those forces are most likely to win, but if they permit the mind to act with death, the forces of death are most certain to win.

So long as one continues to persist in living, refusing absolutely to give into death, they are throwing the full power of mind, thought and will on the side of life. They thereby increase the power of life, and may increase that power sufficiently to overcome death. Again we say that it is a question how many times a person could overcome death by this method, but the fact remains that this method alone can save life repeatedly in the majority of cases; and all will admit after further thought on this subject that the majority will be very large.

This is a method, therefore, that deserves the best of attention in every sickroom. No person should be permitted to die until all available methods for prolonging life have been exhausted, and this last mentioned method is one that will accomplish far more than most of us may expect; and its secret is found in the fact that whenever we give in to any condition or action, it becomes stronger, due to the tendency of the subconscious to enlarge, increase and magnify whatever it receives.

Give in to the forces of death, and the subconscious mind will increase the powers of that force. Give in to the forces of life, and the subconscious mind will increase the power of your life and you will continue to live.

Concerning the general possibilities of the subconscious, we should remember that every faculty has a subconscious side, and that it becomes larger and more competent as this subconscious side is developed. This being true, it is evident that ability and genius might be developed in any mind even to a remarkable degree, as no limit has been found to the subconscious in any of its forces.

In like manner, every cell in the body has a subconscious side, and therefore, if the subconscious side of the personality were developed, we can realize what improvement would become possible in that field.

There is a subconscious side to all the faculties in human nature, and if these were developed, we understand how man could become ideal, even far beyond our present dreams of a new race. It is not well however to give the major portion of our attention to future possibilities. It is what is possible now that we should aim to develop and apply, and present possibilities indicate that improvement along any line, whether it be in working capacity, ability, health, happiness and character can be secured without fail if the subconscious is properly directed.

To direct the subconscious along any line, it is only necessary to desire what you want and to make those desires so deep and so persistent that they become positive forces in the subconscious field. When you feel that you want a certain thing, give in to that feeling and also make that feeling positive. Give in to your ambitions in the same manner, and also to every desire that you wish to realize. Let your thought of all those things that you wish to increase in any line get into your system, because whatever gets into your system, the subconscious will proceed to develop, work out and express.

In using the subconscious, we should remember that we are not using something that is separated from normal life. The difference between the individual who makes scientific use of the subconscious and the one who does not, is simply this; the latter employs only a small part of their mind, while the former employs the whole of their mind. And this explains why those who employ the subconscious intelligently have greater working capacity, greater ability and greater endurance. In consequence they sometimes do the work of two or three people, and do excellent work in addition.

To train the subconscious for practical action is therefore a matter of common sense. It is a matter of refusing to cultivate only a small corner of your mental field when you can cultivate the entire field.

Chapter 9

Chapter IV

of

Christian Larson's "Your Forces And How To Use Them"

(1912)

Training The Subconscious For Practical Results

WHEN you have made up your mind what you want to do, say to yourself a thousand times a day that you will do it. The best way will soon open. You will have the opportunity you desire. If you would be greater in the future than you are now, be all that you can be now. He who is his best develops the power to be better. He who lives his ideals is creating a life that actually is ideal. There is nothing in your life that you cannot modify, change or improve when you learn to regulate your thought. Our destiny is not mapped out for us by some exterior power; we map it out for ourselves. What we think and do in the present determines what shall happen to us in the future.

When we proceed to train the subconscious along any line, or for special results, we must always comply with the following law: The subconscious responds to the impressions, the suggestions, the desires, the expectations and the directions of the conscious mind, provided that the conscious touches the subconscious at the time. The secret therefore is found in the two phases of the mind touching each other as directions are being made; and to cause the conscious to touch the subconscious, it is necessary to feel conscious action penetrating your entire interior system; that is, you should feel at the time that you are living not simply on the surface, but through and through. At such times, the mind should be calm and in perfect poise, and should be conscious of that finer, greater something within you that has greater depth than mere surface existence.

When you wish to direct the subconscious to produce physical health, first picture in your mind a clear idea of perfect health. Try to see this idea with the mind's eye, and then try to feel the meaning of this idea with consciousness, and while you are in the attitude of that feeling, permit your thought and your attention to pass into that deep quiet, serene state of being wherein you can feel the mental idea of wholeness and health entering into the very life of every atom in your system. In brief, try to feel perfectly healthy in your mind and then let that feeling sink into your entire physical system.

Whenever you feel illness coming on, you can nip it in the bud by this simple method, because if the subconscious is directed to produce more health, added forces of health will soon begin to come forth from within, and put out of the way, so to speak, any disorder or ailment that may be on the verge of getting a foothold in the body.

Always remember that whatever is impressed on the subconscious will after a while be expressed from the subconscious into the personality; and where the physical conditions that you wish to remove are only slight, enough subconscious power can be aroused to restore immediate order, harmony and wholeness. When the condition you wish to remove has continued for some time, however, repeated efforts may be required to cause the subconscious to act in the matter. But one thing is certain, that if you continue to direct the subconscious to remove that condition, it positively will be removed.

The subconscious does not simply posses the power to remove undesirable conditions from the physical or mental state. It can also produce those better conditions that we may want, and develop further those desirable conditions that we already possess. To apply the law for this purpose, deeply desire those conditions that you do want, and have a very clear idea in your mind as to what you want those conditions to be.

In giving the subconscious directions for anything desired in our physical or mental makeup, we should always have improvement in mind, as the subconscious always does the best work when we are thoroughly filled with the desire to do better. If we want health, we should direct the subconscious to produce more and more health. If we want power, we should direct the subconscious not simply to give us a great deal or a certain amount of power, but to give us more and more power. In this manner, we shall secure results from the very beginning.

If we try to train the subconscious to produce a certain amount, it might be some time before that amount can be developed. In the meantime, we should meet disappointment and delay, but if our desire is for steady increase along all lines from where we stand now, we shall be able to secure, first, a slight improvement and then added improvement to be followed with still greater improvement until we finally reach the highest goal we have in view. No effort should be made to destroy those qualities that we may not desire. Whatever we think about deeply or intensely, the subconscious will take up and develop further.

Therefore, if we think about our failings, shortcomings or bad habits, the subconscious will take them up and give them more life and activity than they ever had before. If there is anything in our nature therefore that we wish to change, we should simply proceed to build up what we want and forget completely what we wish to eliminate. When the good develops, the bad disappears. When the greater is built up, the lesser will either be removed or completely transformed and combined with the greater.

That the subconscious can increase your ability and your capacity is a fact that is readily demonstrated. Whenever the subconscious mind is aroused, mental power and working capacity are invariably increased sometimes to such an extent that the individual seems to be possessed with a super human power. We all know of instances where great things were accomplished simply through the fact that the individual was carried on and on by an immense power within them that seemed to be distinct from themselves and greater than themselves; but it was simply the greater powers of the subconscious that were aroused and placed in positive, determined action. These instances, however, need not be exceptions.

Any individual, under any circumstances, can so increase the power of their mind, their thought and their will as to be actually carried away with the same tremendous force; that is, the power within them becomes so strong that they are actually pushed through to the goal they have in view regardless of circumstances, conditions or obstacles.

This being true, we should arouse the subconscious no matter what it is we have to do. No day is complete unless we begin that day by making alive everything that we possess in our whole mind, conscious and subconscious.

Whenever you have work to do at some future time, direct the subconscious to increase your ability and capacity at the time specified, and fully expect the desired increase to be secured. If you want new ideas on certain studies or new plans in your work, direct the subconscious to produce them and you will get them without fail. The moment the direction is given, the subconscious will go to work along that line; and in this connection, we should remember that though we may fail to get the idea desired through the conscious mind alone, it is quite natural that we should get it when we also enlist the subconscious, because the whole mind is much greater, far more capable and far more resourceful than just a small part of the mind.

When demands are urgent, the subconscious responds more readily, especially when feelings at the time are also very deep. When you need certain results, say that you must have them, and put your whole energy into the "must." Whatever you make up your mind that you must do, you will in some manner get the power to do.

There are a number of instances on record where people were carried through certain events by what seemed to be a miraculous power, but the cause of it all was simply this . . that they had to do it, and whatever you have to do, the subconscious mind will invariably give you the power to do. The reason for this is found in the fact that when you feel that you must do a thing and that you have to do it, your desires are so strong and so deep that they go into the very depths of the subconscious and thus call to action the full power of that vast interior realm.

If you have some great ambition that you wish to realize, direct the subconscious several times each day and each night before you go to sleep, to work out the necessary ways and means; and if you are determined, those ways and means will be forthcoming. But here it is necessary to remember that we must concentrate on the one thing wanted. If your mind scatters, sometimes giving attention to one ambition and sometimes to another, you will confuse the subconscious and the ways and means desired will not be secured. Make your ambition a vital part of your life, and try to feel the force of that ambition every single moment of your existence. If you do this, your ambition will certainly be realized. It may take a year, it may take five years, it may take ten years or more, but your ambition will be realized.

This being true, no one need feel disturbed about the future, because if they actually know what they want to accomplish, and train the subconscious to produce the idea, the methods, the necessary ability and the required capacity, all these things will be secured.

If there is any condition from which you desire to secure emancipation, direct the subconscious to give you that information through which you may find a way out. The subconscious can. We all remember the saying, "Where there is a will there is a way," and it is true, because when you actually will to do a certain thing, the power of the mind becomes so deep and so strong along that line, that the entire subconscious mind is put to work on the case, so to speak; and under such circumstances, the way will always be found.

When you put your whole mind, conscious and subconscious, to work on any problem, you will find the solution. If there is any talent that you wish to develop further, direct the subconscious every day, and as frequently as possible, to enlarge the inner life of that talent and to increase its brilliancy and power. When you are about to undertake anything new, do not proceed until you have submitted the proposition to the subconscious, and here we find the real value of "sleeping over" new plans before we finally decide.

When we go to sleep, we go more completely into the subconscious, and those ideas that we take with us when we go to sleep, especially those that engage our serious attention at the time, are completely turned over, so to speak, during the period of sleep, and examined from all points of view. Sometimes it is necessary to take those ideas into the subconscious a number of times when we go to sleep, as well as to submit the matter to the subconscious many times in the day during the waking state, but if we persevere, the right answer will finally be secured.

The whole mind, conscious and subconscious, does possess the power to solve any problem that may come up, or provide the necessary ways and means through which we can carry out or finish anything we have undertaken. Here, as elsewhere, practice makes perfect. The more you train the subconscious to work with you, the easier it becomes to get the subconscious to respond to your directions, and therefore the subconscious mind should be called into action, no matter what comes up; in other words make it a practice to use your whole mind, conscious and subconscious, at all times, not only in large matters, but in all matters.

Begin by recognizing the subconscious in all thought and in all action. Think that it can do what you have been told it can do, and eliminate doubt absolutely. Take several moments every day and suggest to the subconscious what you want to have done. Be thoroughly sincere in this matter; be determined; have unbounded faith, and you can expect results; but do not permit the mind to become wrought up when giving directions. Always be calm and deeply poised when thinking out or suggesting to the subconscious, and it is especially important that you be deeply calm before you go to sleep.

Do not permit any idea, suggestion or expectation to enter the subconscious unless it is something that you actually want developed or worked out, and here we should remember that every idea, desire or state of mind that is deeply felt will enter the subconscious. When there are no results, do not lose faith. You know that the cause of the failure was the failure of the conscious to properly touch the subconscious at the time the directions were given, so therefore try again, giving your thought a deeper life and a more persistent desire.

Always be prepared to give these methods sufficient time. Some have remarkable results at once, while others secure no results for months; but whether you secure results as soon as you wish or not, continue to give your directions every day, fully expecting results. Be determined in every effort you may make in this direction, but do not be over-anxious.

Make it a point to give special directions to the subconscious every day for the steady improvement of mind, character and personality along all lines. You cannot give the subconscious too much to do because its power is immense, and as far as we know, its capacity limitless. Every effort you may make to direct or train the subconscious, will bring its natural results in due time, provided you are always calm, well balanced, persistent, deeply poised and harmonious in all your thoughts and actions.

Chapter 10

Chapter VI

of

Christian D. Larson's "How To Stay Young"

(1906)

Training the Subconscious to Produce Perpetually the Elements of Youth

THE subconscious mind has the power to keep the body in health, youth and vigor for any length of time. The subconscious mind is the source of every quality, condition, characteristic, tendency, desire, element or power that appears in the human personality; and as a source it is inexhaustible; therefore, when man learns to draw upon his subconscious source, he may increase any power, perpetuate any condition, or perfect any quality to the highest imaginable degree.

The subconscious can do and will do whatever it is properly impressed or directed to do ; it is therefore evident that any person may, through the proper direction of his subconscious mind, produce youth in his system now, and perpetuate that youth for as long a time as he may desire. Whatever the present condition of the body may be, the subconscious can remove that condition so that the new body that nature has recently produced may appear as it is . . full of health, youth and vigor.

The subconscious mind is the inner side of the whole mind of man; the conscious mind is the outer side. The conscious mind is the wide-awake mind, the subconscious is the interior depths of mentality.

The conscious mind is the thinker, the subconscious is the doer. The conscious mind gives directions, the subconscious carries them out. The conscious mind is the sower, the subconscious is the mental soil . . inexhaustible in the richness of its productive power. The ideas, the thoughts, the beliefs, the desires and the aims of the conscious mind are mental seeds, and when these are deeply felt they will enter the subconscious, invariably producing fruits after their kind.

To train the subconscious to produce the elements of youth, only those ideas, thoughts, beliefs and desires should be entertained in the conscious mind that are conducive to youth and perpetuation of youth.

It is not possible for any state, condition, element or power to be expressed in the human personality until its cause has been formed in the subconscious.

All causes are held and worked out in the subconscious. The conscious mind originates the cause, the subconscious takes it within itself and evolves the natural effect.

All causes are subconscious, and all subconscious causes bring forth their effects into the outer mind and body. Therefore, the subconscious cause of youth must be established before youth will express itself in the personality. The subconscious mind of the child contains the active cause of youth, and also the inactive, latent cause of old age.

The former cause is produced by the natural renewing process, and so long as this cause is permitted to act youth will appear in the personality. The latter cause is inherited from the race ; it is the age producing race habit, and according to the tendencies of its own inherent nature, will begin to produce the old-age condition at the expiration of a period of thirty, forty or fifty years.

To perpetuate youth it is therefore necessary to remove the subconscious age-producing cause that has been inherited from the race; and to remove this cause the entire subconscious mind must be trained to produce perpetually the elements of youth. All age-producing causes will disappear from the subconscious when the entire subconscious mind is permeated with youth-producing causes, and this is our object in view.

To promote this object, the conscious mind must proceed systematically and thoroughly to re-create the subconscious in all its phases; the subconscious must be directed to do everything that is necessary to produce and perpetuate youth, and every subconscious tendency to the contrary, must be displaced by a youth-producing tendency.

To proceed, the subconscious should daily be impressed with the fact that you are young now. What you impress upon the subconscious, the subconscious will express in mind and body; therefore, when the subconscious is deeply and thoroughly impressed with the fact that you are young now, it will produce and express throughout your system the elements of youth now. You will consequently feel young and look young, and you should, because you are young.

When the subconscious is impressed with the fact that you are young now it will cease to follow the race tendency to interfere with the natural renewing process, but will instead, work in harmony with this process, thus removing from the system every age producing habit or tendency that has been inherited from the race.

To impress the subconscious with the idea that you are young now is not to present to the inner mind some imaginary idea; you are young now; it is no theory; your entire system has been made new within the last few months; therefore, permeate your mind through and through with the very spirit of that great truth.

To try to impress an idea upon the subconscious that you know to be untrue is to fail; the subconscious will only accept those ideas that you inwardly feel to be absolutely true. The subconscious will not obey the doubting mind, but the mind of faith and conviction can make the subconscious do anything within its power to do, and To try to impress an idea upon the subconscious there are no limitations, neither is there any end.

To live in the conviction that you are young now is to constantly direct the subconscious to make you look young now, feel young now, and express, through and through your system the vigor of youth now. The subconscious can; the subconscious can do and will do whatever it is properly directed to do.

What the subconscious has been properly and thoroughly trained to do it will continue to do for an indefinite period, or until the conscious mind gives directions to the contrary. Therefore, when the subconscious has been trained to produce the elements of youth, it will continue to produce these elements perpetually, thus insuring continuous youth for that individual so long as he may live upon this plane.

When the subconscious mind has been trained to produce perpetually the elements of youth, it will not only produce these elements in its own personality, but will transmit the youth-producing tendency to the next generation.

When both parents have eliminated from their subconscious minds the age-producing race habit, and have permanently established instead the subconscious youth-producing process, their children will be born absolutely free from the age-producing habit of the race.

Such children will not be born with the habit of growing old, but will be born with a strong subconscious tendency to stay young as long as they may live. Such children will never grow old unless they acquire the habit, later on in life, through the misuse of their own minds. To transmit to their children the perpetual youth producing tendency, it is necessary for the parents, however, to permanently establish this tendency in their own subconscious minds before the conceptions of those children are to take place.

It is the law that whatever the parents have established in their own subconscious minds, they will transmit to their children; the possibilities of parenthood are therefore immeasurable, and to those who understand the unfoldment of these possibilities, then parenthood there is no greater greatness.

The Subconscious minds of all persons, whether they be octogenarians, or in their teens, contain the age-producing tendency; young parents will therefore transmit this growing-old race habit to their children just as readily as those parents that have begun to show the signs of age; for this reason, all persons who expect to become parents must completely remove this race habit from their subconscious minds before they can transmit the youth-producing tendency to their children.

Those parents who succeed only partly in removing the age-producing process from their systems, will give their children the power to retain the vigor of youth for a longer period than the average; but all parents can succeed completely in this respect, and all should proceed with that determination in mind.

Every effort to direct the subconscious to do what we desire to have done, should be promoted in the firm conviction that the subconscious can. To have absolute faith in the subconscious is to reach the inexhaustible powers of the subconscious, and when these powers are reached there is no object in view that cannot be accomplished.

To properly impress any idea or desire upon the subconscious, the conscious mind must not only be firmly convinced that the idea is true, but must keenly feel the nature and the purpose of that idea; and there is no attitude of mind that will promote these two essentials as thoroughly as faith. Every effort therefore that is made in the training of the subconscious should be permeated with strong invincible faith.

The fact that the body is being constantly renewed makes it possible for the subconscious, not only to perpetuate the elements of youth in the body, but also to constantly improve everything in the human personality.

Therefore, when the subconscious is being directed to produce the elements of youth, it should also be directed to produce the elements of beauty and physical perfection. Impress upon the subconscious the most perfect idea of physical beauty that the mind can possibly conceive, and desire with deep feeling, that the elements of that beauty be produced and expressed through every atom of the physical form.

In like manner, direct the subconscious to build for yourself a finer and a finer personality, a stronger character and a more brilliant mind. And always proceed in the faith that the subconscious can. Whenever you think of yourself, mentally see yourself as the picture of health, youth and vigor, and introduce into that picture the most perfect idea of physical beauty that you can possibly imagine.

This picture should be daily impressed upon the subconscious; that is, while holding the picture in mind, think of the subconscious with deep feeling, and try to feel that the elements of the picture are being appropriated by the subconscious. Every mental picture that is properly impressed upon the subconscious will be reproduced in the human system, because whatever is impressed upon the subconscious will be developed and expressed in the personality.

To mentally live in the world of this picture will aid remarkably in bringing the nature of the picture into the subconscious, and this is especially true when the mind pictures itself in the world of health and youth. To mentally live in a certain state or attitude is to take that state or attitude into the subconscious. That which we live we invariably impress upon the subconscious; therefore to perpetually live in the spirit of youth is to cause the subconscious to perpetually create the elements of youth.

To live in the belief that you are growing older every year is to direct the subconscious to make you feel older and look older every year; and this is what nearly every person is doing, though principally through the force of habit . . race habit. He is there by training his subconscious mind to produce old age; but it is just as easy for the subconscious to produce perpetual youth if properly directed to do so.

When the subconscious is trained to produce youth, and express youth throughout the entire personality, it will cease to produce conditions of old age, and will consequently interfere no more with the perpetual renewing process; instead, it will promote that process.

To remove the tendency of the hair to change its color at those periods when race thought expects it to change, direct the subconscious to perpetuate the natural color of the hair. The fact that the color of the hair has already begun to turn gray need not cause anyone to hesitate to apply this method.

The actions of the mind can produce chemical changes in the physical system; to restore the natural coloring matter of the hair would be no more difficult for nature than the healing of a wound; but changes and modifications in human nature can be produced only through the subconscious, therefore, the subconscious must first be directed to do what we wish to have done.

To direct the subconscious to perpetuate the natural color of the hair, picture this color as clearly as possible in mind ; then, with deep feeling, impress the soul of this picture upon the subconscious; that is, place your thought in the very soul, or inner life of that color, and impress that thought upon the depths of subconscious life. To mentally live in the absolute faith that the subconscious is perpetuating the natural color of the hair is sufficient where the color has not begun to change; but where the change has begun, special attention must be given to the matter daily to restore normal conditions. To retain the natural color of the hair it is also necessary to avoid strenuous mental action, hard thinking, forced thinking, nervousness, worry, fear and similar adverse mental states.

This is also true with regard to the perpetuation of youth throughout the system; all mental states must be harmonious, and all physical conditions wholesome.

To secure harmonious mental states and wholesome physical conditions, all that is necessary is to direct the subconscious to produce them; the subconscious can.

To direct or impress the subconscious with the positive assurance of securing the desired results, there are three fundamental essentials to be closely observed. First, the idea to be impressed should be clearly discerned in mind; second, when concentrating this idea upon the subconscious, the mind should act in the attitude of the deepest possible feeling; and third, the real existence of the subconscious mind itself should be felt in every part of the personality.

The subconscious mind occupies the entire personality and fills every atom with its finer mental life; in fact, it is an immense, inner, mental world that permeates every part of the being of man; therefore, when trying to impress an idea upon the subconscious, attention should be concentrated upon the finer life that permeates the outer life.

When the conscious mind feels the finer life of the subconscious mind, the thought of the conscious mind IS in contact with the power of the subconscious, and whatever the conscious mind, during this contact, may desire to have done, the subconscious will proceed to do.

This contact is always produced when the conscious mind is in an attitude of deep feeling, and this deep feeling will invariably follow the combined action of faith and desire .

. the desire to impress the subconscious, and the absolute faith that the subconscious can do whatever it is impressed to do.

Chapter 11

Chapter VIII

of

Abel Leighton Allen's "The Message of New Thought"

(1914)

As A Man Thinketh

"Mind is the master-power that molds and makes,
And man is mind, and ever more he takes
The tool of thought, and shaping what he wills,
Brings forth a thousand joys, a thousand ills:
He thinks in secret, and it comes to pass:
Environment is but his looking-glass." - JAMES ALLEN

NATURE does not thrust powers and accomplishments upon us. In her infinite wisdom she left us a work to perform. Endowed by Nature with incipient powers, it was left to man to develop them or not, as he should determine.

Wisely was it ordained when man was created that he should eat his bread by the sweat of his brow. Labor has been the propelling force in man's progress and advancement in civilization. Without it he would have placed no value on that which satisfies his wants and ministers to his comforts. We value that most which we accomplish by our own efforts, either physical or mental. "Diamonds are found only in the dark places of the earth; truths are found only in the depths of thought," says Victor Hugo.

That we may have a due appreciation of the forces and powers within us, we must learn to unfold and develop them for ourselves. This we can do only by the exercise of our own thought and will power. If we wish mental power, we can have it only as we exercise the faculties of the mind and thus develop and educate them for the work that devolves upon us. If we wish character, thought is the key to its development. If we desire accomplishment along any chosen line, we must put forth the thought and effort necessary to produce the sought-for results. If we wish to utilize the subjective forces within, only as we properly train the objective mind to play upon them and impress its thought upon them can we expect valuable or important effects.

Cause and effect are written everywhere in the universe. The law of compensation is ever before our eyes. If we would evade it, it steps in our pathway to block our progress. We must ever pay the price. Wherever there is an effect, there was first a cause.

Everything in the universe that we observe, all the varied and marvelous manifestations in Nature, all that takes place in men's lives, proclaim the truth and universality of this law. From elections to worlds keeping their orbits through infinite space, all things animate and inanimate must obey the positive mandates of this law. This law is as inexorable, unerring, and constant in the mental and spiritual planes as in the physical universe. It is never suspended, never varies; it is fixed and eternal.

The same law that the planets obey, that causes the seed to germinate and grow, that brings the recurring seasons with equal precision regulates and controls every thought sent forth from the human mind. Let us consider well what thoughts we entertain, and how we shall send them forth, for they are causes and will in good time come into expression in our own lives. As a man thinketh in his heart, so is he. This wondrous truth is old, and it is new. Its application is new to us every moment of our lives. Its real significance and true meaning were never known until the discovery of modern psychology.

Until we have learned something of the nature of subconscious mind, we can have but a faint understanding of the import of this golden proverb. We must first realize that the subconscious mind has control of the functions and forces of the body; that it is the great mental and spiritual storehouse of man; that it is amenable to every suggestion of the objective or conscious mind; "that the conscious mind acts, the subconscious reacts; the conscious mind produces the impression, the subconscious produces the expression; the conscious mind determines what is to be done, the subconscious supplies the mental material and necessary power," before we can understand its full meaning and significance.

Translated into modern language, we would say that as a man thinks deeply and reaches down into the subconscious mind and impresses it with his thought the subconscious mind will respond according to the nature of the thought and impression. Plato said: "Thinking is the talking of the soul with itself." Thought is dynamic. Thoughts are not things, but the forces back of things; the creators of things. Thought is power, thought is force, thought is cause.

"Our todays are the result of our past thinking, our tomorrows the result of our present thinking. We have been our own mental parents, and we shall be our own mental children. All that a man does and brings to pass is the vesture of thought."

There is a correspondence between thought and deeds, thoughts and circumstances. Thoughts produce conditions in our physical bodies, in our lives and circumstances, according to the character of those we harbor. Emerson says: "The key to every man is his thought. Sturdy and defying though he look, he has a helm which he obeys, which is the idea after which all his facts are classified. He can only be reformed by showing him a new idea which commands his own,"

Every thought accompanied with deep feeling, or impressed upon the subconscious mind, produces chemical changes and effects upon the body. Thoughts of fear and anxiety disturb the functions of the body and bring weakness and disease. Pleasant, agreeable, and joyful thoughts bring health, strength, and poise.

"The pleasantest things in the world are pleasant thoughts, and the greatest art in life is to have as many of them as possible."

The laws of mind are fixed, absolute, and eternal. We are the results of the sum total of our thinking. Thoughts are revealed in our faces and manifested in our lives. As we glance in the mirror, we see the reflection of our thoughts. Men foolishly believe their thoughts are their own, and that they may entertain them in secret and keep them to themselves. Thoughts are not secrets; they are not their own. Every thought is registered in the archives of the soul. Thought pencils the lines in the brow. Thought plows furrows in the cheek. Thoughts reveal their character in the expression of the eye. The face is the mirror, reflecting the mind and thought of its possessor.

Walt Whitman says:

"Sauntering the pavement or riding the country road, lo! such faces.

Faces of friendship, precision, caution, suavity, ideality!

The spiritual prescient face--the always welcome common benevolent face.

The sacred faces of infants, the illuminated face of the mother of many children.

The face of an amour, the face of veneration.

The face withdrawn of its good and bad, the castrated face;

This now is too lamentable a face for man;

Some abject louse, asking leave to be cringing for it.

This face is a haze more chill than the Arctic sea;

Its sleepy and wobbling icebergs crunch as they go.

The melodious character of the earth,

The finish beyond which philosophy cannot go, and does not wish to go,

The justified mother of men."

If we but observe, we too can see the faces Whitman saw, as we saunter through the highways and byways of life. Similar faces appear in every street and thoroughfare. Whitman looked through the eyes of the seer, he saw beyond the faces, he recognized the silent causes there registered, he understood. We, too, can look beyond the expression to the cause and understand they were all wrought in the forge of thought. We can almost feel the calculating thought of the man with a face "A haze more chill than the Arctic Sea." We can see a life of unselfish love back of the face of "The justified mother of men."

The character of thought betrays itself, not only in the faces of men, but in their lives and characters as well. Thought determines character. Thought is character. James Allen has well said: "Think good thoughts and they will quickly become actualized in your outward life, in the form of good conditions. Control your soul forces, and you will be able to shape your outward life as you will. The difference between a saviour and a sinner is this, that the one has a perfect control of all the forces within him; the other is dominated and controlled by them.

> "Dwell in thought upon the grandest,
> And the grandest you shall see;
> Fix your mind upon the highest,
> And the highest you shall be."

What we sow, that shall we also reap. Some men seem to think this law applies only to outward acts and relates only to the sowing in a physical world. But the same law governs mind and thought.

Thoughts of revenge, hatred, jealousy, envy, and lust affect and mold the character and lives of those who harbor them as certainly as effect follows cause. Sooner or later they will be externalized and manifested in every outward circumstance and condition of life.

Thoughts generate health or toxins in the system according to the kind of thought entertained. Thoughts of malice, fear, hatred, and envy interfere with the normal functions of the body, affect its secretions, generate poisons, resulting in disease. Thoughts of health, thoughts of joy, thoughts of kindness, bring joy and health to him who entertains them and sends them forth.

If we think ourselves inherently bad, we shall reap the fruits of that thought. If we conceive of ourselves as weak and unworthy, as Whitman said, "Asking leave to be," we shall develop those qualities and actualize them in our daily lives. If we recognize divine attributes as our inheritance, we shall grow into the likeness of those attributes. Whitman said: "I believe in you, my soul--the other I am must not abase itself to you. To me the converging objects of the universe perpetually flow."

It is the man of conscious power within that wins in life's contest. He is great, because his thought was first great. The man who is conscious of the potentialities of his own nature and couples energy with that thought, is master of circumstances. He is the magnet that attracts power, attracts success; he is success. A man may have a lofty opinion of himself but as long as he thinks small thoughts he will be small. Man can only become great as he thinks great thoughts, and to think great thoughts he must seek to gain a larger consciousness of real worth and superiority.

Greatness is strength, without egotism. It is power, with a desire that others shall not recognize that power. Jesus said, "Blessed are the meek, for they shall inherit the earth." He did not employ the term "meekness" as the synonym of "weakness." His thought was that man should be great without parading it, without ostentation: strong without letting it be known. This is the essence of all greatness.

By the law of suggestion the subconscious mind is amenable to the thoughts and impressions it receives from the conscious or objective mind. The subconscious registers the impression which is again given expression in the life and character of the individual. The subconscious faithfully reproduces every mental idea or state contained in the impression. The law is as unerring as the law of gravitation. As is the suggestion, so is the result.

The subconscious is a rich soil, and the seed thought planted therein by the conscious mind will produce according to its kind. If we plant flowers, we shall pluck flowers. If we sow tares, the crop will be tares. The subconscious is an obedient servant. It obeys the thoughts of the conscious mind. What it receives, it reproduces, and its effect is manifested in the personality of the individual. If we sow ideas of diseases, we shall reap a harvest of disease. Thoughts of health will be re-expressed in healthful conditions. If we sow ideas of poverty, that will be our portion. If we sow thoughts of inferiority, weakness, and fear, we shall build a personality devoid of character and strength. Ideals of abundance will produce abundance, if we plus them with intelligence and energy.

In that valuable little volume "The Great Within," Mr. Christian D. Larson has stated the law well and correctly. "The subconscious mind is a rich mental field: every conscious impression is a seed sown in the field, and will bear fruit after its kind, be the seed good, bad, or otherwise. All thoughts of conviction and deeply felt desires will impress themselves upon the subconscious and will produce their kind, to be later expressed in the personal being of man."

Since the subconscious is impressed with every earnest and deeply felt thought, it is easy to understand how beliefs stamped upon youthful minds are perpetuated in adult age, whether they are true or false. The subjective mind receives them in an impressionable age, and there they remain and grow throughout the years of life. Certain institutions understand the psychological law perfectly and therefore insist on what they call religious instruction in early life, before they encounter any opposition from auto-suggestion or independent thought. The religious instruction usually consists of teaching certain creeds and dogmas, and in most instances playing upon the emotions to cause their teachings to be impressed upon the subconscious. Fear has been the favorite influence to cause these impressions to become permanent in the subconscious.

These impressions, being ground into the subjective mind, remain to bring forth fruit after their kind in the succeeding years. It is no evidence of their truth that they remain as fixed belief in mature age. Men believe what was impressed on the subconscious mind in early life, because that belief has become so firmly planted therein that it becomes a habit. Habits thus formed in childhood prevent the mind from accepting any line of thought that does not accord with those habits or beliefs. They are accepted as fundamentals, and logic and reason are powerless to overcome them. Yet these habits and beliefs, however firm or fixed they may become, may or may not be true. That they are thus believed in mature life, by men of the highest intellectuality, is no evidence of their truth.

Men of greatest mental attainments differ as widely in their religious beliefs as the opposite poles of the universe. They cannot all be true. The question is asked, Why do intelligent men differ so radically? The explanation lies in a study of psychological law, that the subconscious mind is so thoroughly impressed in childhood that the impression is never eradicated, but remains a fixed and permanent habit and belief through life. Men are compelled to believe as they do by reason of the deep impression on the subconscious mind. These impressions are so strong that they color and warp everything that enters into the mind thereafter, even education itself. Thus education and training become merely servants of our earlier beliefs.

Then, too, ecclesiastical authorities and ecclesiastical reverence are important factors in silencing youthful minds from questioning what they are told. They are taught that they must accept the instruction given, as the final commands of authority, and to make further inquiries would tempt the divine patience. These become deep and lasting impressions on the subconscious mind, the tendencies of which are to preclude further inquiries in later years.

As long as the world continues to cling to the idea that some men are clothed with exclusive authority to teach truth, or that their authority cannot be questioned, so long will they be able to fasten beliefs upon the human mind that reason and judgment cannot dislodge or eradicate.

So long as the child is taught that it is dangerous to think except as his spiritual advisers tell him and that he must accept their interpretation of what has been written, so long will he refuse to see or accept truth or enlarge his conceptions of truth. Whatever his intellectual attainments may be, he is likely to remain a spiritual slave. Mr. Larson has well said, "When you accept anything as final, you bring your mind to a standstill in that sphere of action; and the fact that nearly the whole world has accepted certain spiritual ideas as final is the reason why spirituality . . real, living spirituality . . is almost unknown today."

The conscious mind supplies the ideals for the subconscious mind to work to and bring forth into expression. This is a subject for the deepest thought and consideration, and is the key to all true mental training. As is the ideal, so will be the expression. It is of the utmost importance that proper and truthful ideals be always held before the subconscious, for whatever they are they will find expression in the life, character, and personality of the individual.

Chapter 12

Excerpt from

Chapter V

of

Abel Leighton Allen's "The Message of New Thought"

(1914)

Universal Mind in Man

MAN is discovering the forces and powers of the great soul within; better than all, it has found the law by which man can unfold, develop, and control these forces and make them obedient agencies of his will.

Man is realizing that the great subconscious mind is an infinite storehouse of intelligence and power, and that when he has learned the laws by which it is reached, impressed, and controlled, he may draw from its inexhaustible depths at will to supply his needs and wants. He is coming into the consciousness that the great subconscious, "the Great Within," his own masterful soul, is the link that unites him with the Great Divine Soul. He is learning that the subconscious controls the functions of the body, its life, its growth, and the entire physical organism, and that every thought of the objective mind is a power that will affect the subconscious and the entire personality of man.

Psychology reveals that the laws of mind and thought are absolute and changeless, that the subconscious will respond to whatever thought is impressed upon it. When man has come into a realization of this truth. and learned to control his thoughts and impress the subconscious only with constructive, healthful, and worthy thoughts, he has learned the secret of transmuting thought into power, life, and health, and thus revolutionizing his entire life and being. When he has reached that understanding and has come into possession of that secret, he has found the kingdom of God within, which is the kingdom of mind.

When the kingdom of mind rules man's life, he has found his own center, he has acquired power and poise, he is no longer swayed and buffeted by the caprices and whims that ever disturb the thoughtless; he lives his own life as nature designed it, the storms of discontent and anxiety are stilled within, he expresses in his life the beauty, the harmony, and power of the kingdom of God within.

Chapter 13

Chapter XIII

of

Charles M. Simmons "Your Subconscious Power, How To Make It Work For You"

How to Use the Power of Your Subconscious

HOW many times, in the most recent years of your life, have you experienced a sense of power? Not often enough, I venture to suggest, and then it probably was a vicarious experience. You can remember moments of having this feeling of power from the time you were a youngster. Memories of those earlier years include times when you skated, rode a bike, a coaster wagon or a sled and you pushed yourself until you were going faster and faster. For a moment or two, your speed would be so excessive that you were just on the edge of being scared. But, my, what a sense of power it gave you!

- **A new kind of personal power**

Such moments had more grown-up flavor to them in your 'teen years. Perhaps the sense of power came when you shot a rifle for the first time, or when you were the starring participant in competitive games, when you were the "big" sister or brother to some "little kids."

All of these incidents came from environmental opportunities, a sense of power coming from the outside. There was no lasting quality to it. A transition of this kind of power to adult years is sought by some people, but it is nothing to be recommended. Some people, for example, get behind the wheel of a car and induce a momentary sense of power by seeing how high they can push the speedometer and get away with it. The feeling of power fades as the car slows down. No one is entitled to this kind of power. However, everyone seeks some sense of personal power, because it is a form of recognition of ourselves. There is a kind of personal power you should seek in acknowledgment of your importance to yourself.

- **You have used this power at times**

As an adult, you have already had some manifestations of this kind of power. You may not have sought it because you didn't know how, but each time it came to you, it had a lingering, desirable after-effect. And each time it came, it came from within you, not from the outside.

If you are a mother, this sense of power came to you at the birth of your child. You had the feeling that you had surpassed any other accomplishment in your whole life by being an instrument of the ultimate in creativeness. The power of creativeness gave you a transcending feeling of personal power. Perhaps, like thousands of men and women, you have had religious experiences that have caused a welling up of courage and strength within you. Perhaps, like many others, you are able to renew this sense of personal power consistently.

There have been times when the acquiring and the possession of knowledge has given you that sense of inner power. These have been times when specific knowledge has made you better prepared and more confident in the face of a specific requirement in life. Sense of power from this source is inherent in your experience with this book.

And there should have been times in your life when a sense of power came because of the effect of your influence on other people. We have already discussed the existence of negative power by which some persons usurp the lives of others. You, of course, have never been, or ever will be, a supporter of this kind of power. But there have been times, I am sure, when your influence has powerfully and positively affected the lives of others and you have rightfully felt that inner, personal power.

- **This power was demonstrated just yesterday**

Your "biography" would undoubtedly record many such manifestations of feeling this inner sense of power; if your personal history is up-to-date, it will record that you had such an experience just yesterday and that you are still feeling the effects of it. Just yesterday (if you have been faithfully using your book as a guiding light), you made that demonstration to yourself of the effectiveness of your subconscious in creating a positive attitude. Today you have a clear, bright picture of your plans, which gives a sense of readiness to put them into action. This readiness gives a sense of power, the power to act, the power over circumstances and environment, as these might affect your plans. This power came from within you. It was created through the work of your subconscious and it is maintained as a feeling of power by your subconscious.

- **Only one source of inner power**

The same basic pattern that covers your experience of yesterday and today covers all of the experiences you have had with the feeling of inner power. The feeling of power seemed to well up from nowhere. In each case there was action involved, but it was all physical or mechanical conscious action, intrinsically resembling many other actions in your life which did not bring on this sense of power. You didn't press a button and suddenly have this power turned on! There is no such button that anybody can press. You can't force this power to appear. You can only let it appear, after you have set the stage with proper conscious preparation. Only the power of your subconscious can bring this desired feeling of inner power to you.

Was this as true with the other experiences in your life as it was with the one you were guided into yesterday? The answer is "yes." With a mother, the physical preparation of pregnancy and the physical act of giving birth are overtoned by her love and anticipation of the coming child. This love and anticipation grows as her period of pregnancy advances. Her subconscious mind is anticipating the birth as well as is her body. With the child finally in her arms, her subconscious lets that love literally overflow and turns that anticipation into fulfillment. Without that subconscious preparation, the birth could be as emotionally devastating as it is physically arduous. The power of the sense of fulfillment was already within her, subconsciously. She had only to let it be felt.

- **Inner power from knowledge**

The acquiring of knowledge, of course, is related to books, classes, courses or experience. Possibly only a relatively small portion of what you have learned through these processes has given you a feeling of power. When it did happen, it was not the "facts" that you had learned that in themselves gave you this feeling; it was the personal use you related them to. It happened when you related them to a goal or objective and particularly when you anticipated the use of them during the learning process. It happened when you were motivated to learn by saying to yourself: "These facts, in my possession, will enable me to do a certain something better." Thus, while the memory "departments" of your subconscious were helping you assimilate the facts, other "departments" were remembering your high anticipation of their use. With the facts acquired, your subconscious played back that anticipation in the form of satisfying accomplishment and that sense of personal inner power.

- **Strength from inner power**

So it is with church attendance, or with prayer. These acts seem to bring about passive reactions. But the repetitious relationship with them also conditions your subconscious mind. When, at some time in your everyday life, you have the need for courage and strength beyond the normal, your subconscious will remind you that the source of this courage and strength lies in your faith. Your subconscious was storing up this inner power so that you could feel it at the time you needed it most.

And so it is in your relationships with others. When you act to be of service to others, those subconsciously stored traits of graciousness and understanding influence your actions. Your subconscious intentions are of the best and the other person responds accordingly. The fact that your influence affects another person gives you a sense of personal power, but it comes about only because of the release of that positive subconscious power to act graciously and with understanding.

- **How to turn on inner power**

There is one fundamental difference between experiences such as these and the recent one concerning your plans. It is that the latter was done with great deliberateness, with one hundred per cent predetermination of the results! And that is the secret of using the power of your subconscious, by deliberate preparation and by conscious predetermination of the outcome. Beyond that, you do nothing; you can do nothing to cause its power to be a major factor in your life. And this brings us to the first and only time we shall consider anything like a "formula" or "rules and regulations."

I did not dream up this formula. Science did not invent it, although science can be credited with discovering it. When the Creator gave you that two-part mind of yours—the conscious and the subconscious—He made this formula "part and parcel" of the fact that you are a human being. The formula has three steps to it.

1. Deliberately condition your subconscious by what you do consciously. You are always aware of what you are doing. Apply a personal "golden rule" to this awareness. "Do unto your subconscious as you would have your subconscious do unto you." That is why the recording camera is in your mind.

2. Wholeheartedly want the best results from such self-influence action. Certainly this supports the creed of "do" that is now yours. This is why that priority "filing system" exists in your subconscious.

3. Let your subconscious have free reign in demonstrating its power. Let things happen to you and they will happen to you. That is why you have your will at the control panel in your mind.

The use of this formula will bring the power of your subconscious mind into full play. It is the only way to use it positively, and the word "positive" is the only thing that I would add to this formula. Of course, I don't know why anyone would want to be deliberate about negative conditioning, or would want, or let, negative outcomes be predominate, least of all you!

- **Go on a retreat to start right**

Now we can add some practical "do it yourself" suggestions to this formula. You have heard of the "retreat" program that many churches have. Perhaps you have had the remarkable experience of attending one. In such an experience, a person spends many consecutive hours in silent contemplation with himself and the spirit of his Creator and, in a practical fashion, with his subconscious. The objective is for him to see himself, and his life, objectively. Frankly, the best way to make steps one and two of the formula most effective is to go to a "retreat" in preparation for them. The time you spend alone, if only a few minutes, in contemplation of deliberate action will start you off on the right track without the slightest doubt. Try to establish a pattern of brief but regular "retreats" in your daily life.

- **Avoid trial-and-error ideas**

Don't use the trial-and-error method of finding the right material for your subconscious to work on. There is no need for you to do it. This pattern of action is a time and effort waster and unnecessarily delays achievement. Seek guidance, if you are uncertain of the best steps to take at any time. Books, courses, counseling, the experience of others are all resources for supplying yourself with usable knowledge. With such proven knowledge, you will follow the positive course of self-influence.

Your subconscious is a versatile powerhouse. It can, and is willing to, work on many actions and results at the same time. Give it the chance to work for you at its top capacity by having a variety of positive actions on your program at any one time. In fact, the more you use the power of your subconscious, the more it will appear to be a power in your life. Before you are through with your book, you will realize that here is one certain instance where practice makes perfect.

• Be positive! Be deliberate!

Deliberate guidance, positive guidance, is the key to using the power of your subconscious. The best use of this power is dependent upon this guidance. So strongly do we believe in this, at the Simmons Institute, that we guide students of our home study course into the ultimate in deliberate, positive self-guidance. We provide them with the tools for the guided influence of their subconscious minds, while they sleep. This guidance is directly related to the subject matter of the course. This is an extension of the type of experience you had, in relation to Chapter 11 of your book.

• Use your tireless subconscious

You know now, of course, that this is possible because the subconscious mind does not sleep . . does not need sleep. You know that it is willing to be influenced while you sleep. Because we help our students take advantage of this, their relationship with the course is stepped up immeasurably. Like them, I know you will take advantage of every opportunity offered you in the practice steps to increase the power of your subconscious, by influencing it while you sleep.

Chapter 14

Chapter III

of

Thomas Parker Boyd's "The Mental Highway"

(1922)

Conscious, Subconscious and Superconscious

THE mind in action is conscious, subconscious and superconscious. We are aware of all conscious activity. We are aware of some subconscious activities expressed in our dreams, mingled with our conscious mentation, and in the functional operations of our bodies. The vast part of subconscious activity never rises to the plane of consciousness.

We know superconscious activity as it expresses in our dreams, in a vision, and consciously as a special illumination. The superconscious must express all its operations in symbolism, symbols created by the conscious and subconscious. Apart from these symbols, we cannot intelligibly describe the things known in superconscious.

We may cease to be conscious of the feelings and experiences of life anytime because of the weakness of their individual elements, because the connection between them ceases, or because sleep or some artificial hypnotic inhibits them. They continue unconsciously until the inhibition passes or else the activities of life break down the body because of lack of conscious oversight. A physical stimulus may take effect without any sensation, as when food arrives in the stomach, exciting the flow of gastric juice, starting peristaltic motion, and starting the liver and pancreas. Yet we are aware only of the mechanical part of this process, the chewing and swallowing, and the general feeling of satisfaction that results.

We may have ideas and experiences of which we are, at the time, largely unconscious. For instance you may be unconsciously in love. You do not know it. However, everyone else does, and eventually it emerges into your consciousness.

Memory furnishes another field in which to observe the action of the conscious and the subconscious. Memory reproduces mental images of experiences and ideas. These seem to be lost, but we store up their impressions. Often they spring up spontaneously, at other times we recall them by a little conscious effort and association, while very often they refuse to come into consciousness no matter how much we may try to recall them.

Then we resort to the time-honored device of turning the attention to other things, and a subconscious trigger causes the memory-image to emerge into mental view.

We often study some problem, gather a mass of facts about it, attempt to set them in order, and the conscious effort ends in confusion and disorder. When we abandon the conscious effort, the subconscious, which has been at work all the time, has a chance to project into consciousness a perfect plan or outline of the subject, which is a logical deduction from the main facts. If we fail to solve a problem, we lie down to sleep, and in the dream state the subconscious can reveal the solution, which it has already grasped.

In the act of hearing, the passing of the vibration through the half dozen steps of transmission to the brain are all unconscious, yet they are an integral part of the process of hearing and classifying of sound, which is a conscious action.

We never really become aware of many subconscious links in all conscious work. A proposition, which we learned to understand by means of proof, remains long after we forget the proof itself. Most of the things we believe are bare outlines, the reasons for which we have forgotten, if we ever knew them.

Many conscious ideas arise from some subconscious decision as, for instance, those qualities classed as instinct, tact, etc. Selfish tendencies often persist after the first causes have passed away. A person begins to drink to drown trouble and continues drinking, unaware that his motive has subconsciously shifted. His only possibility for a cure will be by discovering a motive powerful enough to hold him, and by arousing his will power to carry that motive into effect.

Conscious motives pass, but their effects remain in the subconscious. Instinct acts for ends of which we are not conscious at all. Conscious efforts leave behind them subconscious effects. Four hundred years of the spirit of Egypt had so permeated the subconscious life of Israel that it required generations to eradicate it. It takes more than one generation to erase the effects of slavery from the consciousness so that one will not wince at the crack of the whip.

It is also true that what one does mechanically may eventually gain complete control over the conscious and the subconscious, and he will do the thing wholeheartedly. Take a person whose whole habit of life has been pessimistic and depressed, and who is accustomed consequently to being weak and ill. Let him start in the most mechanical way to affirm the positive side of life (joy, hope, and love), and very soon it will sink into his conscious and subconscious. The new habit will change his whole mental and physical condition.

We may also conceive and carry conscious and subconscious processes simultaneously. We can do any automatic task while carrying on a totally different mental process, and be totally oblivious to what our fingers are doing. Knitting is a good example.

This interplay of conscious and subconscious is ever present in our life of thought, emotion and action. Things that move us profoundly have large elements of subconscious ideation in them. Much of the emotional activities like love, hope, and faith, is subconscious. The subconscious facts and processes lie below all the sharply defined conscious processes, merely waiting some shock or movement to project them into full consciousness.

The study of the dream state, intermediate between the conscious and the subconscious, is instructive. Dreams may reveal the connection between our sleeping and waking states, and the relations of the conscious and subconscious. In all our dreams we may usually discover some relation between the substance of our dream and the facts of the waking state, either recent or remote.

The subconscious is always connected with the conscious world by touch, sound and the other senses. A soldier can sleep in the midst of a battle, yet will awaken at a whispered signal. A mother will sleep soundly, yet will awaken at the first movement of her child. We may set our mind to awaken at a certain hour, and sleep undisturbed until then. These all illustrate the interplay of conscious and subconscious activity in our waking and sleeping states.

Analyzing a person's dreams will often detect the presence of a hatred for or fear of some person or thing, or the unsuspected influence of some past act, which fills the life with disharmony, bringing ills to both body and mind.

Expecting very much improvement will be useless until they consciously remember these secret states and acts; the very explanation of such conditions will often begin the cure. We need to address any idea that begins to assume prominence in sleeping or waking states, at once.

Chapter 15

Chapter III

of

Charles F. Winbigler's "Suggestion, its Law and Application, or, The Principal and Practice of Psycho-Therapeutics"

(1919)

The Relation of Suggestion to the Subconscious Mind

THE relation of suggestion to the subconscious mind may be rudely stated as that of key and lock. The power by which this mind will open and reveal its treasures is suggestion. We give again the description of the subconscious mind, as it is very important that these characteristics shall be recognized in this stage of the discussion.

The subconscious mind governs and controls all of the vital functions of the body automatically, and its highest powers are instinct or intuition, faith, spiritual perception, telepathic power, clairvoyant ability, and at times absolution from physical or bodily limitation, and it is also the seat of the emotional life and perfect memory.

The most remarkable manifestations of knowledge and power occur when the conscious mind is held in check. Suggestion is the key that unlocks the door into the real individual life and lets us get a glimpse into the wealth, power, and possibilities of the subconscious mind.

The Secrets, Mysteries & Powers of The Subconscious Mind

The influence of the subconscious mind over the nutrition and health of the physical system has been recognized by thinking men generally, but has never been so widely discussed as at the present time. For instance, in victory and defeat of armies nutrition is affected favorably or unfavorably. Dr. Austin Flint said to a medical class some years ago : "Gentlemen, there is something in the practice of medicine far beyond the mere administration of drugs." He told a great truth.

Every successful physician knows the necessity of controlling the patient's mind. He knows the value of faith, hope, expectancy, and belief, and that they are among the most powerful therapeutic agents that c n be used. The scriptural statement, "Thy faith hath made thee whole," is thoroughly scientific, and if we carefully observe, we shall find many verifications of this truth. Hope, one of the greatest powers in the human mind, is at once elevating, uplifting and inspiring. Physically hope can accelerate the heart action, relieve the nerve tension, and bring into one's life great benefits.

Fear, on the other hand, depresses the nerve action, contracts the blood vessels of the body, and interferes with the circulation. It also produces mental depression, and, very speedily, physical ailment. When man has learned thoroughly the difference between hope and fear, he has discovered one of the greatest principles of healing. When he has learned how to encourage and inspire hope, how to dispel despondency and drive away fear, he has discovered an effective method of relieving the afflicted of many ailments.

Take, for instance, a man who is in an excellent physical and mental condition and let him receive a report that his house has burned down, that some of his dear ones have lost their lives, and see how quickly it will produce a depressing effect and illness. If he were to receive news five or six hours after, that it was a mistake, that the property was intact and the loved ones safe, his illness would leave him almost instantly.

If he had consulted the doctors after receiving the news of disaster, and had not informed them of it, they would have attributed his collapse and illness to different causes. Some would probably have said that this condition was caused by ptomaine poisoning; some would have attributed the cause to overwork; others would have blamed it on a severe cold, and probably others on different physical conditions. Various remedies would have been recommended. The real cause was a thought or thoughts which produced a shock, and as long as these were entertained the physical results would continue.

Adverse suggestions had entered the subconscious mind and were depressing the vital functions; and, as long as they controlled, depression of the circulatory and nervous systems would result.

When the safety of home and loved ones became assured, the normal condition was reestablished, the arteries relaxed, the pallor was replaced by a glow of red in the face, the nerve action became normal, and the usual health was realized, with the happiness that followed therefrom. He was made ill by a thought of fear, he was cured by a thought and an assurance of safety. The thoughts we think, the exercise of faith in God and man, the inspiration of hope, all have a definite effect on every cell in the human body.

The helpless and sick infant is soothed by the mother's loving fondling, her tenderness of touch and voice are lodged in the child's mind, rest and sleep follow and recovery from sickness. The sick man who goes to see the doctor is examined and wisely informed that he has a serious illness, but that he can be readily cured by taking the medicine prescribed. He swallows the drastic drug and soon begins to feel much better.

He believes the medicine (larvated suggestion) has done the work, whereas the examination and the assurance of the doctor were the secret of cure through the vital functions of the organic life. Bread pills or other things in the Materia Medica could have been just as efficiently used as the medicine which was prescribed and taken. We are coming to a time when this wonderful law of suggestion will be as generally used as medicines have been, and perhaps more effectively and less deleteriously.

It is conceded by the best psychologists that cognition, reasoning, and volition are the fruitage of the conscious mind, also that feeling, perfect memory, and extraordinary mental phenomena, have their initiative in the subconscious mind. These manifestations arise into the plane of consciousness, so that in memory we have recollection and the action of the law of association on that plane.

Suggestion is related to the law of similarity and association. The best way to train our memories and deeply impress them is by the relations of inclusion, exclusion, and concurrence. This work is effectually done in the conscious sphere, and permanently received and retained in the subconscious mind.

This mind, especially the emotional features of it, is marvelously affected by suggestion. The power of choice, which may be called the law of preference, is the characteristic of the conscious mind, but when desire and feeling enter into the matter, then the power of the deeper mind is brought into play. Here is the explanation of many cures and peculiar things in man's life.

> "Lulled in the secret chambers of the brain,
> Our thoughts are linked by many a hidden chain,
> Awake but one, and lo! what myriads arise,
> Each stamps its image as the other flies."

There is a very essential, if not vital, relation between the subconscious mind and the suggestion which it receives.

The leaders of the Nancy School of Hypnotists have observed and stated that it is by suggestion that hypnotic phenomena are produced and subjects are controlled. This is confirmed by thousands of cases and has been established inductively as a law.

It has brought into view a large field of observation, and a wide series of phenomena, ordinary and extraordinary, so that it has become a new method of explaining unusual mental phenomena, which have puzzled physicians, jurists, learned and thoughtful men.

Suggestion is a special kind of psycho-physical reaction in which an idea or thought becomes so intense and limited that the mind becomes possessed with one idea. This idea loses for the time its ordinary associations and influence and breaks through ordinary restrictions and liberates cerebral activities which seem to belong to a deeper mind. Suggestion produces a dissociation of feelings, desires, and volitions which are ordinarily associated.

Where the mental power of dissociation is easy, the person is readily suggestible. For instance, a person is wide awake, yet I suggest that he is sleepy and that he feels like yawning and he becomes drowsy and then yawns. I hold out his arm and tell him that he cannot move it up or down and he is unable to do so. He is in an hypnotic or suggestible condition. Suggestion and hypnotism, in a special sense, are identical, but in a large sense are not so. Hypnosis is a graduated sleep, induced by suggestion.

The sleep also increases the power of suggestion. The mental mechanism and results are of the same sort, but differing in degree according as one is awake or asleep. In sleep, the dissociation is more general than in the waking condition, in which it is partial and limited. Suggestion, as to its present effective influence, comes principally from other people, but may also come from environment, books, things, emotions, extraordinary manifestations, etc., or from one's own conscious mind.

Suggestion in this special sense has opened up a new world of mystery. This world has been called "the involuntary mind," "unconscious cerebration," "the subliminal self," "the subjective mind," "the unconscious mind," "the subconscious mind." We are only on the shore of this soul-sea. Pebbles have been gathered and classified, and the partial nature and fragmentary contents of this sea have been seen, tabulated, and analyzed.

Suggestion is the power by which we may open and explore this vast and hitherto unseen and not understood world, and it is also the power by which we may bring forth order, usefulness, and help for humanity. The power which modifies suggestions from an operator, and sometimes makes them utterly ineffective, is the auto-suggestion of the subject's mind. This is an element that must always be reckoned with by the operator or healer. There are times when such persons are nonplused because of the ineffectiveness of their suggestions, even though they had been previously able to get excellent results in the hypnotized or passive subject.

The conscious mind of the subject has been giving the subconscious mind auto-suggestions which have nullified the power of the operator or healer. The reason for the subject doing this may be found in the fact that he was told that he did certain unbecoming things when hypnotized. He then says to himself, "I will not do those things again," and as a result the experiments are failures while the person is in the hypnotic condition. Auto-suggestion did it.

There have been numerous efforts to prove the existence of two minds, with varying success, from Plato to Hudson. This does not interest us now, but we use the phrase "conscious mind" as applied to that mental power which deals with external conditions of life and the phrase "subconscious mind" as applying to the essential, enduring and mysterious self.

The subconscious mind has, under certain conditions, the power of clairvoyance, clairaudience, kinetic and telepathic energy. The conscious mind uses the cerebro-spinal nervous system and is dependent largely upon that as an instrument of manifestation, but the subconscious mind seems to manifest its phenomena and power independently of, and at times contrary to, the working of the brain and spinal nerves. It probably uses directly the sympathetic nervous system and has an independent functioning entity or force.

Ordinarily and normally, man is controlled by reason, knowledge, and the evidence of the senses. When suggestions from others appeal to him he usually gives assent. But when he is in a passive or hypnotic condition he is controlled by the influence of another, and often contrary to reason and knowledge. The stronger suggestion will prevail. This is philosophical, because we find that man under the influence of hypnosis is more than an unreasonable, irresponsible manikin, as some persons would have us believe. He has inherent power by which he can break the spell which may lead him to do unvirtuous acts which are contrary to his moral education.

This confirms our view that suggestion is the power by which the subconscious mind is controlled by another, and auto-suggestion is the inherent power by which the influence of another is counteracted and nullified.

Suggestions lodged in that mind can effect a complete change, morally and physically. If mankind could become in spirit "as a little child," trusting in God implicitly, the greatest power would be utilized in the establishment of health and equilibrium, and the results would be untold in comfort, sanity, and blessing. For instance, here is one who is suffering from worry, fear, and the vexations of life. How can he get rid of these things and relieve this suffering?

Let him go to a quiet room or place, twice a day, lie down and relax every muscle, assume complete indifference to those things which worry him and the functions of the body, and quietly accept what God, through this law of demand and supply, can give. In a few days he will find a great change in his feelings, and the sufferings will pass away and life will look bright and promising. Infinite wisdom has established that law; and its utilization by those who are worried and fearful will secure amazing results in a short time.

The reader may ask how this is secured. The explanation is not far to seek. The physical system has been on a severe strain, owing to depressing effects of worry and fear, and has come almost to the point of breaking. Its nervous equilibrium has been greatly disturbed and the depressed condition has affected the heart action, the digestion, and the vital functions.

When the person becomes quiescent, and relaxes the muscles by an act of the will and persistent passivity, the nerves have a chance to regain their normal, healthful action, all the functions of the body commence to work naturally, the health is restored, and the unreasonableness of fretting, fearing, and worrying becomes so apparent that the afflicted one sees the foolishness of that course of life and gives it up.

The real reason for the change is found in the possibility of recovery by using the laws that God has placed within our reach, and thus securing the coveted health and power for all that we want and ought to do. The subliminal life is the connecting link between man and God, and by obeying His laws one's life is put in contact with Infinite resources and all that God is able and willing to give.

Here is the secret of all the cures of disease and the foundation for the possibility of a joyful existence, happiness, and eternal life. Suggestion is the method of securing what God gives, and the mind is the agent through which these gifts are received. This is not a matter of theory, but a fact. If anyone who is sick or who desires to be kept well will have stated periods of relaxation, open-mindedness, and faith, he can prove the beneficial and unvarying result of this method.

Chapter 16

Chapter I

of

Neville Goddard's "Feeling is the Secret"

(1944)

Law and its Operation

THE world, and all within it, is man's conditioned consciousness objectified.

Consciousness is the cause as well as the substance of the entire world. So it is to consciousness that we must turn if we would discover the secret of creation.

Knowledge of the law of consciousness and the method of operating this law will enable you to accomplish all you desire in life. Armed with a working knowledge of this law, you can build and maintain an ideal world.

Consciousness is the one and only reality, not figuratively but actually.

This reality may for the sake of clarity be likened unto a stream which is divided into two parts, the conscious and the subconscious. In order to intelligently operate the law of consciousness, it is necessary to understand the relationship between the conscious and the subconscious. The conscious is personal and selective; the subconscious is impersonal and non-selective. The conscious is the realm of effect; the subconscious is the realm of cause.

These two aspects are the male and female divisions of consciousness. The conscious is male; the subconscious is female.

The conscious generates ideas and impresses these ideas on the subconscious; the subconscious receives ideas and gives form and expression to them.

By this law . . first conceiving an idea and then impressing the idea conceived on the subconscious . . all things evolve out of consciousness; and without this sequence, there is not anything made that is made. The conscious impresses the subconscious, while the subconscious expresses all that is impressed upon it. The subconscious does not originate ideas, but accepts as true those which the conscious mind feels to be true and, in a way known only to itself, objectifies the accepted ideas.

Therefore, through his power to imagine and feel and his freedom to choose the idea he will entertain, man has control over creation.

Control of the subconscious is accomplished through control of your ideas and feelings.

The mechanism of creation is hidden in the very depth of the subconscious, the female aspect or womb of creation.

The subconscious transcends reason and is independent of induction. It contemplates a feeling as a fact existing within itself and on this assumption proceeds to give expression to it.

The creative process begins with an idea and its cycle runs its course as a feeling and ends in a volition to act.

Ideas are impressed on the subconscious through the medium of feeling. No idea can be impressed on the subconscious until it is felt, but once felt . . be it good, bad or indifferent . . it must be expressed.

Feeling is the one and only medium through which ideas are conveyed to the subconscious. Therefore, the man who does not control his feeling may easily impress the subconscious with undesirable states.

By control of feeling is not meant restraint or suppression of your feeling, but rather the disciplining of self to imagine and entertain only such feeling as contributes to your happiness.

Control of your feeling is all important to a full and happy life. Never entertain an undesirable feeling, nor think sympathetically about wrong in any shape or form. Do not dwell on the imperfection of yourself or others. To do so is to impress the subconscious with these limitations. What you do not want done unto you, do not feel that it is done unto you or another. This is the whole law of a full and happy life. Everything else is commentary.

Every feeling makes a subconscious impression and, unless it is counteracted by a more powerful feeling of an opposite nature, must be expressed. The dominant of two feelings is the one expressed. I AM healthy is a stronger feeling than I will be healthy. To feel I will be is to confess I am not; I AM is stronger than I am not.

What you feel you are always dominates what you feel you would like to be; therefore, to be realized, the wish must be felt as a state that is rather than a state that is not.

Sensation precedes manifestation and is the foundation upon which all manifestation rests. Be careful of your moods and feelings, for there is an unbroken connection between your feelings and your visible world.

Your body is an emotional filter and bears the unmistakable marks of your prevalent emotions. Emotional disturbances, especially suppressed emotions, are the causes of all disease. To feel intensely about a wrong without voicing or expressing that feeling is the beginning of disease . . disease . . in both body and environment.

Do not entertain the feeling of regret or failure for frustration or detachment from your objective results in disease.

Think feelingly only of the state you desire to realize. Feeling the reality of the state sought and living and acting on that conviction is the way of all seeming miracles. All changes of expression are brought about through a change of feeling. A change of feeling is a change of destiny. All creation occurs in the domain of the subconscious.

What you must acquire, then, is a reflective control of the operation of the subconscious, that is, control of your ideas and feelings.

Chance or accident is not responsible for the things that happen to you, nor is predestined fate the author of your fortune or misfortune.

The Secrets, Mysteries & Powers of The Subconscious Mind

Your subconscious impressions determine the conditions of your world. The subconscious is not selective; it is impersonal and no respecter of persons. The subconscious is not concerned with the truth or falsity of your feeling. It always accepts as true that which you feel to be true.

Feeling is the assent of the subconscious to the truth of that which is declared to be true. Because of this quality of the subconscious there is nothing impossible to man.

Whatever the mind of man can conceive and feel as true, the subconscious can and must objectify. Your feelings create the pattern from which your world is fashioned, and a change of feeling is a change of pattern.

The subconscious never fails to express that which has been impressed upon it. The moment it receives an impression, it begins to work out the ways of its expression. It accepts the feeling impressed upon it, your feeling, as a fact existing within itself and immediately sets about to produce in the outer or objective world the exact likeness of that feeling.

The subconscious never alters the accepted beliefs of man. It out pictures them to the last detail whether or not they are beneficial.

To impress the subconscious with the desirable state, you must assume the feeling that would be yours had you already realized your wish. In defining your objective, you must be concerned only with the objective itself.

The manner of expression or the difficulties involved are not to be considered by you. To think feelingly on any state impresses it on the subconscious. Therefore, if you dwell on difficulties, barriers or delay, the subconscious, by its very non-selective nature, accepts the feeling of difficulties and obstacles as your request and proceeds to produce them in your outer world.

The subconscious is the womb of creation. It receives the idea unto itself through the feelings of man. It never changes the idea received, but always gives it form. Hence the subconscious out pictures the idea in the image and likeness of the feeling received.

To feel a state as hopeless or impossible is to impress the subconscious with the idea of failure.

Although the subconscious faithfully serves man it must not be inferred that the relation is that of a servant to a master as was anciently conceived. The ancient prophets called it the slave and servant of man.

St. Paul personified it as a "woman" and said: "The woman should be subject to man in everything."

The subconscious does serve man and faithfully gives form to his feelings. However, the subconscious has a distinct distaste for compulsion and responds to persuasion rather than to command; consequently, it resembles the beloved wife more than the servant.

"The husband is head of the wife,"

may not be true of man and woman in their earthly relationship but it is true of the conscious and the subconscious, or the male and female aspects of consciousness.

The mystery to which Paul referred when he wrote,

"This is a great mystery... He that loveth his wife loveth himself... And they two shall be one flesh,"

is simply the mystery of consciousness.

Consciousness is really one and undivided but for creation's sake it appears to be divided into two.

The conscious (objective) or male aspect truly is the head and dominates the subconscious (subjective) or female aspect. However, this leadership is not that of the tyrant, but of the lover. So, by assuming the feeling that would be yours were you already in possession of your objective, the subconscious is moved to build the exact likeness of your assumption.

Your desires are not subconsciously accepted until you assume the feeling of their reality, for only through feeling is an idea subconsciously accepted and only through this subconscious acceptance is it ever expressed.

It is easier to ascribe your feeling to events in the world than to admit that the conditions of the world reflect your feeling. However, it is eternally true that the outside mirrors the inside.

"As within so without."

"A man can receive nothing unless it is given him from heaven,"

and

"The kingdom of heaven is within you."

Nothing comes from without; all things come from within .. from the subconscious.

It is impossible for you to see other than the contents of your consciousness. Your world in its every detail is your consciousness objectified. Objective states bear witness of subconscious impressions. A change of impression results in a change of expression.

The subconscious accepts as true that which you feel as true, and because creation is the result of subconscious impressions, you, by your feeling, determine creation. You are already that which you want to be, and your refusal to believe this is the only reason you do not see it.

To seek on the outside for that which you do not feel you are, is to seek in vain, for we never find that which we want; we find only that which we are.

In short, you express and have only that which you are conscious of being or possessing.

"To him that hath it is given."

Denying the evidence of the senses and appropriating the feeling of the wish fulfilled is the way to the realization of your desire.

Mastery of self-control of your thoughts and feelings is your highest achievement.

However, until perfect self-control is attained, so that, in spite of appearances, you feel all that you want to feel, use sleep and prayer to aid you in realizing your desired states.

These are the two gateways into the subconscious.

Chapter 17

Chapter VII

of

W. John Murray's "Mental Medicine"

(1923)

The Subconscious Mind

IN the science of mind it is doubtful if anything of greater importance has been brought to light than that vast submerged storehouse of memories which modern psychologists speak of as the subconscious mind. One likens it to that infinitely greater portion of an iceberg which is under the water, while all that appears is a more or less scanty surface. Another speaks of it as that great depth of the ocean of mind which maintains its perpetual calm despite the turbulence which may be occurring on the surface; while another speaks of it as a sort of phonographic disk, which receives impressions only to repeat them again when proper conditions are provided for the repetition.

Innumerable instances are on record to prove that, independent of the conscious mind, the subconscious mind may receive impressions which it will carry out with infallible exactitude. It is because of this that hypnotized subjects, when all conscious objections to the absurdity of things are inhibited, carry out those suggestions which are made to them and which cause them to act as if they were swimming on dry land and climbing up ladders where no ladders exist. These phases of undoubted phenomena would be of no real value in themselves were it not for the fact that they point to something higher and more useful than themselves.

We know that the conscious mind of the individual is the smallest part of the thinking entity and that it is largely, if not exclusively, limited to that form of information which reaches it through the avenue of the senses, while the subconscious mind is open to impressions from three sources. First of all it is impressed by what is conveyed to it by objective things; then it is impressed by what reaches it from that stream of thought which is spoken of as "race belief;" and then again it is impressed by those thoughts which have been generated by all the high and holy thinking of the spirits of "just men made perfect."

We are told that the subconscious mind never initiates; that is, it never starts any train of reasoning on its own account; but follows whatever is conveyed to it from any of the sources above mentioned. This is why it has been likened to a phonographic disk which receives impressions only to give them back again on demand, and this whether these impressions are harmonious or discordant; for the office of the subconscious mind is not to select but to serve.

When this is better understood we shall be more careful of the thoughts we think and the suggestions we permit to find their way through the conscious mind into the subconscious. We shall be on our guard against the suggestions which come to us from what we see, such as advertisements of patent medicines, which not infrequently cause the susceptible to fancy they have the malady for which the patent medicine is recommended; from what we hear in the form of conversations about recent operations; and what we read in the papers concerning deaths, divorces and disasters of various names and natures.

Physicians will be more careful and considerate concerning their all too frequently outspoken diagnosis of certain cases as "incurable," especially within the hearing of the patient. One day it will be considered unethical to look hopeless in the presence of an invalid. A physician's smile of encouragement will be worth more than all his drugs to his patient, while his increased success in the art of healing will undoubtedly add to his income. A hint to the wise in the profession is sufficient.

Older physicians have seen their so-called incurables get well and remain well so often that they are somewhat loath to use the word incurable any longer. Materia medica is not the last word, for there is that mysterious thing the doctors call vis medicatrix natura which does strange and unaccountable things, amazing the doctors as well as delighting their patients.

Vis medicatrix natura may be only another name for that which the modern psychologist calls race subconsciousness; that vast reservoir which contains all the thoughts of the race since time began; just as individual subconsciousness contains all the forgotten as well as remembered thoughts of the individual. What we call instinct in the sick animal, which causes it to select such food and herbs as make for restoration, may be nothing other than general subconsciousness welling up to meet some particular need.

Animals and young children do not oppose subconscious promptings as a rule. Adults reason themselves away from these suggestions as a result of the bias of an education, which has not, until recently, taken the subconscious into consideration. And yet, see what great things are attributable to its processes!

The most vital processes of man's organism are controlled by subconscious thought. It is the subconscious which forms bones, nerves, and muscles, and reforms them as old cells give place to new ones. It is the subconscious mind which governs circulation, assimilation, digestion, breathing, etc. It is to subconscious processes that the action of the liver, lungs, and heart are due. Why should not man learn to cooperate consciously with the subconscious? Is it that he has persuaded himself that this is not possible, or may it be that he has never given any thought to it at all?

We do not feel that it is enough for us to have a muscular system. We are convinced that this muscular system needs to be exercised in order to retain its vigor and elasticity, and we do this exercising consciously and deliberately. We do not feel that it is enough for us to be provided with intellectual capacities.

We strive with intellectual capacities. We strive to expand these capacities through study and a keen desire for information, both of which are exercise for the mind, as walking and other things are exercise for the body. In the same way we should not feel that it is enough for us to have a subconscious mind, for unless we make some use of it we might as well not have it.

If you have ever been in a foundry you must have been interested in that part of it which is given over to the casting of things. Here is a huge box in which is kept great quantities of sand, and here are many other boxes, or frames, into which this sand is put in order to receive the impressions of those patterns which hang on the walls.

When these patterns or molds have been made in the sand, the box is then tightly closed, and through an aperture in the top of the box the molten metal is poured, finding its way into the depressions made for it by the patterns.

When the metal has become cold it is taken out in such forms or shapes as the patterns are intended to produce. The pattern of the elephant does not come out as the design of a dog, nor that of the dog as the elephant: each is true to its own particular form. It is the same with consciousness and subconsciousness. Consciousness is constantly pouring liquid thought into the receptive sand of the subconscious mind, and there it assumes the form of the mental picture of perfection, or of imperfection, as the case may be.

The liquid thought of fear will not assume the solid shape of courage; neither will the liquid thought of disease assume the solid form of health; formless thought like formless metal will assume the shape of that into which it is poured.

Every thought we think, if we think it persistently, tends to create the prototype of that which will surely come to pass, unless we reverse the process.

The subconscious "I am ill," it is like an order given to a faithful servant which will be carried out faithfully and at once, or, if you say or even think, "I am well," everything within you will tend at once to carry out this idea. "As a man thinketh in his heart (subconscious mind), so is he" (in his body and in his affairs).

Chapter 18

Chapter IV

of

Venice Bloodworth's "Key To Yourself"

(1952)

The Subconscious Mind

THE subconscious mind presides over all the involuntary processes of your body, such as digestion, assimilation, elimination, the beating of your heart, the circulation of your blood, the manufacture of various glandular secretions. It builds, sustains, repairs and operates the body. Under its direction new cells are born every minute.

So accustomed are we to these operations of the subconscious mind that for a long time science failed to recognize any distinction between our two phases of mind. Finally, however, positive proof of cell renewal directed by a central intelligence presented itself, and it was learned that while the subconscious mind faithfully and tirelessly keeps up its work of building and operating the body whether we are awake, asleep, or under the influence of an anesthetic, it works under the control of the conscious mind.

The subconscious mind is the storehouse of memory, the seat of habit and instinct; it is also the center of emotion, and its action is automatic. The subconscious is that marvelous phase of your mind that brings things into existence by the sheer power of thought. It is the spiritual part of us and through it we are connected with the Divine and brought into relation with Infinite constructive forces of the universe.

The subconscious mind not only possesses the power and knowledge to build and repair your body; it is a part of the Universal Mind and has Infinite resources at its command. Dr. Jung tells us that the subconscious mind not only contains all the classified data gathered during all the past life of the individual, but that it contains also all the wisdom of all the immeasurable ages past, and that by drawing upon its wisdom and power the individual may possess the good things of life in great abundance.

Dr. Jung also makes clear the fact that so long as the individual remains in ignorance of his subconscious power just so long does it remain a great unused force that can prove dangerous to our welfare. Ignorance of the existence and power of the subconscious mind is the cause of all the failures and near failures in the world.

On the other hand we can draw on the subconscious mind for all the wisdom and power necessary in the management of all our business and personal affairs. In fact, anything we leave absolutely to the subconscious mind to handle we will see accomplished.

The subconscious mind does not think, reason, balance, judge, or reject. It simply accepts all suggestions furnished by the conscious mind whether they be good or evil, constructive or destructive. Herein lies the mighty power of the conscious mind. The subconscious mind receives any idea or belief as a pattern to work by and proceeds to bring such ideas and beliefs into manifestation.

Prior to the development of our conscious reasoning power the subconscious mind works by a hereditary pattern, or race instinct. During childhood these subconscious activities are the result of heredity and environment demands and continue to be such unless we are fortunate enough to learn the unlimited power of our subconscious mind, though some people unconsciously draw on this power with most splendid results.

Thus we find the secret of good or bad results in child training is due to the fact that whatever training children get leaves its impression on the subconscious mind and makes the habits formed in our tender years the basis for all future actions unless we consciously and systematically set about to change them.

Every thought that enters the conscious mind is subjected to our reasoning power. If we accept an idea or thought as true, it is then carried to the subconscious mind to act on and is brought forth into the visible expression as part of our physical condition and immediate surroundings.

Thus we find that in its last analysis the conscious mind decides our fate. So to control our health and environment we must control our thought.

Chapter 19

Chapter II

of

Paul C. Ferrell's - "The Subconscious Speaks"

(1932)

Using Conscious Thought in a Definitely Creative Manner

THE subjective mind is exactly what the name implies. It is a subject, or a servant, of the conscious mind of man. It is a servant in the sense that it was created for the use of man. It is entirely at his disposal. All that a man has to do is to command. The Subconscious always obeys. It obeys orders whether consciously or unconsciously given. It is of so sensitive a nature that every thought registers upon it.

The conscious mind is the one and only force to which the Subconscious mind responds. Conscious thought has power. The human concept of power is physical. Power in reality is a product of mind. Mind in all its different phases is God. Mind is Spirit. God is Spirit. Man is Spirit. Recognizing the Unity of all, and claiming this Unity for himself, establishes for man contact with Divinity. Man says: "There is one source from which all things come. The source is God. God is spirit. God is Mind. I am one with the Spirit and Mind of God."

Power is the term by which energy is known to man. Thought energy is the greatest form of energy that exists, for back of thought is mind; and, although mind is back of everything that exists, thought is more closely allied to mind than is any other form of energy. That, in a brief manner, explains why thought has power.

Concentrated thought is more powerful than idle thought. In order for the thoughts of man to make a definite impression upon the Subconscious mind, they must be of sufficient force to register. By force, I mean intensity. Intensity is achieved by concentration. In order to concentrate, stillness and a certain amount of quietude are necessary. That is why you hear so much about the "Silence." It is necessary for effective work. There is nothing mysterious about "going into the silence." It is simply to allow the mind to gather its forces and focus them upon the sensitive plate or negative, to use a photographic term, of the Subconscious mind.

In concentration a man causes his thought force to come to a focus, or central point, and at this point there is a concentration of energy. This can be explained by the illustration of a magnifying glass and the focus it can make of the rays of the sun. It is the difference between scattered vibrations and vibrations which radiate from a focal point. Just as the sun's rays gain in intensity and are able to burn when focused upon a certain place, in like manner thought vibrations . . which are in many respects similar to the rays of the sun . . gain a similar intensity. They make not only a definite but a lasting impression upon the Subconscious mind.

The conscious mind of man is the human dynamo that sends power to the Subconscious mind. It is this dynamic quality which a man should employ to do creative work; and since the conscious mind is the only force to which the

Subconscious responds, a man should understand the manner in which the conscious mind should be used.

The method should be as follows: First, stillness . . then quiet. These are simply to prevent extraneous matters from interfering with the idea which the individual wishes to hold. This idea, or thought, should embody several things. There first must be a desire . . and the more overwhelming the desire, the more definite the impression upon the Subconscious mind. Desire is in reality a form of prayer, if a man realizes that God is the Source of Universal Supply.

After the desire there must be a realization that God's bounty is ever at mankind's disposal. It is this realization that I shall often refer to as Acceptance. It is a mental acceptance, and it is what is meant by the words "What things soever ye desire, when ye pray, believe that ye have them, and ye shall have them."

First is Desire . . then Acceptance. Realization of these first two requisites is essential, for they constitute the basis upon which rests the entire process. After these two things are firmly established in the conscious mind, the rest is easy.

A man should next concentrate upon the thing which he desires. The manner of concentration is this: He should sit quietly and begin to see in his mind the thing which he wants. For example: A man wishes to earn a definite sum of money for a specific purpose. First he should concentrate upon that sum of money. He should see himself in possession of that amount either in gold, silver, currency, or a check made out to himself. He should hold that picture in his mind for a few moments.

He may elaborate the picture in any manner he may choose. He can take the money and open a purse and put it inside. He can see himself depositing it in a bank, . . that is, giving it to the cashier, or doing anything he feels inclined to do. The more earnestly he throws himself into the picture, the more effectually will the picture take hold.

Then he should see himself using this same money to purchase or to pay off the thing he had in mind. If it is an automobile . . to illustrate . . he should see himself going to the show room. He should see himself going through the identical process that he would go through if he were actually buying a car. He can order it delivered, or he can get into it and drive it home. After forming the complete picture, the next thing is to claim this thing for his own, calling himself by name. He then says: "I command the power inherent within me to hold this thought in mental concentration until it is manifested to me."

If he does this with enough conviction that he can do these things; and makes the mental pictures consistently; and keeps it up long enough, the idea, or thought will be impressed upon the Universal mind through his Subjective mind until the manifestation is brought into existence. By existence, I mean into his physical possession.

Suppose a man owes money. His home is mortgaged. He has no manner of raising the money to meet the mortgage. The main thing to do is to stop worrying. That forms a positive blocking of the creative process. He should use his will power and hold in his conscious mind a picture of the house belonging to him, free from all encumbrance. This same picture will register upon his Subconscious mind, and the power inherent within himself will cause to be manifested sufficient funds to meet the indebtedness.

He should say to himself daily: "I am in touch with a power that knows all things . . that is all the power that exists. This power is available to me whether I understand it or not. It is in operation at all times whether I use it or not. It can provide me with everything I need if I call upon it. I now decree for myself the money necessary to meet my every need. The house is now free from encumbrance in the realm of the Universal; and what exists in the realm of the Universal must manifest in the realm of the material."

He should not concern himself with the manner in which these things are to be brought to him. He should do whatever comes his way, and affirm that Divine Mind knows the things necessary for the fulfillment of the things he wants.

Man must have the conviction that he has a power inherent within himself to make a visualization come into manifestation, or he is only wasting his time. There must be an absolute conviction that it is coming to him by virtue of his God-given power to do constructive work with his mind. Just to sit idly and imagine the things he would like to possess will not bring them to him. The idea itself does not do creative work unless there is a strong motive power of thought back of it. Otherwise, all that a person would have to do would be to wish for something. The chief thing to do is to think clearly, to the exclusion of everything else. Then he should take several minutes to let the picture register upon his Subconscious mind.

Often a person desires a thing with such an overwhelming desire that he unconsciously forms a mental picture; and it manifests in a manner approaching the thing which he desires. The thought, in a sense, manifests .. yet it does not manifest of itself alone. The thought always makes an impression upon the Subconscious. The Subconscious imparts this impression to the Great Universal. The Universal always responds.

That is the reason why certain people succeed and why others fail. Certain people know exactly what they want. The Subconscious is then able to carry out their ideas, because their minds have a definite concept of the thing they want accomplished. I am telling you this in order that you may understand the importance of making definite plans. Get a definite mental picture of the thing you desire.

I have stated before that there is a great deal of difference between idle thinking and constructive thinking. Constructive thinking means this: It is knowing that there is an inherent power within man that enables him to use his power of thought to bring into manifestation the thing which he wants. I say wants . . for man is not supposed to live by bread alone. Man may want many things that he does not actually need. That is all right. God has filled the earth with limitless wealth. It was placed upon and under the earth for mankind's enjoyment.

A man should take time each day to decide upon, or make definite statements about what he wants to happen. The words are not so important as the certainty within himself that he has the power and the God-given right to demand whatever he wants or needs.

After a man has decided upon what he wants, he should make a mental picture of having that thing in his possession. Mental pictures always manifest. The reason for this is that it gives the Subconscious something definite to work upon. A picture made by the conscious mind leaves what might be called a negative upon the Subconscious mind; and I think that I shall say that a manifestation is simply a development of that negative. That is a term used in photography, and it is a perfect illustration of the manner in which the conscious mind affects the Subconscious mind. To complete the metaphor . . The conscious mind is the camera . . The

Subconscious is the plate upon which the negative is registered . . The Universal is the pool of liquid in which the negative is immersed, and it is of such a nature that it not only develops the picture, but it also sends that same picture back to the photographer in a material form.

Concentration is necessary. Concentration is the act whereby a mental picture is focused into or through the camera onto the plate of the Subconscious, upon which a negative is registered. The chief thing to remember in this connection is that the Subconscious mind requires, what is called in photographic parlance, a time exposure. The longer the time and the more concentrated the thought . . the more perfect is the picture and the more successful will be the materialization.

An individual is conscious of his conscious mind. He cannot see it, but he knows that he possesses one. He is conscious of himself. It is this Self-knowingness that makes him an individual. Although he cannot see his conscious mind, he accepts the fact without question that he has one. But he does not always accept the fact that he has a Subconscious mind, because he is not conscious of it to the same degree that he is of his conscious mind. The Subconscious mind of man is as much a reality as is his conscious mind. Consider that the conscious mind and the Subconscious mind are realities. Then a proper understanding of the relation the one bears to the other may be the means of supplying mankind's every need.

Man has but to seek and he will find whatever he seeks, whether it be health, wealth, or illumination of any kind whatsoever.

Chapter 20

A Few Excerpts From Various Metaphysical Authors on The Subconscious Mind

Fairy tales .. you will say. And of course, they are. But back of them is more than mere childish fable. There is the Wisdom and the Mysticism of the East .. so frequently hidden in parable or fable.

For those Wise Men of the East had grasped, thousands of years ago, the fundamental fact .. so hard for our Western minds to realize .. that deep down within ourselves, far under our outer layers of consciousness, is a Power that far transcends the power of any conscious mind.

"The Holy Spirit within us," deeply religious people term it. And, truly, its power is little short of Divine.

"Our Subconscious Mind," so the Scientists call it.

Call it what you will, it is there .. all unknown to most of us .. a sleeping Giant who, aroused, can carry us on to fame and fortune over-night, A Genii-of-the-Brain more powerful, more the servant of our every right wish, than was ever Aladdin's fabled Genii-of-the-Lamp of old.

Health and happiness, power and riches, lie ready to its hand. You have but to wake it, to command it, to get of it what you will. It is part of you .. yet its power is limitless. It is Mind .. Thought .. Idea. It is an all-powerful mental magnet that can draw to you anything you may desire.

Robert Collier

The Spiritual Law of Cause and Effect

The startling but very apparent fact is that we do not obtain to the good of life by being moral or righteous alone, but we obtain good by creating good by the power of our faith and thought.

"As ye sow, so shall ye reap" is one of the world's most veiled and misunderstood sayings. For centuries, religious belief has held that Jesus meant that the moral, ethical, and lawful misconduct of a man would be punished in the hereafter. Nothing could be farther from the truth. This saying speaks only of the spiritual law of cause and effect: a seed sown in the garden of the mind shall reap the blossom thereof.

For the Subconscious Mind is a garden, and like the garden of earth that knows only to cause things to grow, the garden of the Subconscious Mind knows only to create reality from the seed of thought. Whether this thought is moral or immoral, ethical or unethical has nothing whatever to do with the inexorable process involved. For the seed having been planted must grow, and grow it will, into physical fact, unless the seed itself is uprooted and another planted in its stead.

U.S. Andersen

Less than 10 per cent of our mental processes are conscious; the other 90 per cent are subconscious and unconscious, so that he who would depend upon his conscious thought alone for results is less than 10 per cent efficient. Those who are accomplishing anything worthwhile are those who are enabled to take advantage of this greater storehouse of mental wealth. It is in the vast domain of the subconscious mind that great truths are hidden, and it is here that thought finds its creative power, its power to correlate with its object, to bring out of the unseen the seen.

Charles F. Haanel

Let us start right now putting into practice some of these truths that you have learned. What do you want most of life right now? Take that one desire, concentrate on it, impress it upon your subconscious mind in every way you can, particularly with pictures. Visualizing what you want is essential, and pictures make this visualizing easier.

Psychologists have discovered that the best time to make suggestions to your subconscious mind is just before going to sleep, when the senses are quiet and the attention is lax. So let us take your desire and suggest it to your subconscious mind tonight. The two prerequisites are the earnest DESIRE, and an intelligent, understanding, BELIEF. Someone has said, you know, that education is three-fourths encouragement, and the encouragement is the suggestion that the thing can be done.

You know that you can have what you want, if you want it badly enough and can believe in it earnestly enough. So tonight, just before you drop off to sleep, concentrate your thought on this thing that you most desire from life. BELIEVE that you have it. SEE it in your mind's eye, and see YOURSELF possessing it. FEEL yourself using it.

Do that every night until you ACTUALLY DO BELIEVE that you have the thing you want. When you reach that point, YOU WILL HAVE IT!

Robert Collier

A man actually is, what he makes the subconscious realm of his mind believe he is. The subconscious realm is that part of a man's mind, which in the Bible is referred to as "The heart." "As he thinketh in his heart, so is he." This is not an opinion, but an inviolable law of God; an absolute statement of fact. The subconscious realm has power within itself to fashion the man according to its own beliefs.

Charles W. McCrossan

Subconscious mind has no volition of its own and only acts on suggestions from your conscious mind or the Source of Wisdom. If you say, "I cannot," the subconscious mind receives the suggestion, assimilates it, and it then becomes a part of you. This connects you with other despondent minds through the quality of your thought, and you feed each other with failures.

One object of autosuggestion is to impress upon your subconscious mind the thought that you can and will, and success follows. This mind also reacts on your conscious mind. If you have been an "I cannot" chap for years, every time you think a vigorous "I can" thought your other self says, "No, you cannot," and depresses you, making your efforts spasmodic and unfruitful. You must first get that mind trained to feel that you can, and it will sustain you if you feel discouraged. This takes time, the length depending on your receptiveness and flexibility. There can be no failure.

Bruce MacLelland

What is back of success? A law as old as the hills, a law that has been known to psychologists for years . . the law that the subconscious mind accepts as true anything that is repeated to it convincingly and often. And once it has accepted such a statement as true, it proceeds to mold the Creative Force working through it in such wise as to MAKE IT TRUE!

You see, where the conscious mind reasons inductively, the subconscious uses only deductive reasoning. Where the reasoning mind weighs each fact that is presented to it, questions the truth or falsity of each, and then forms its conclusions accordingly, the subconscious acts quite differently. IT ACCEPTS AS FACT ANY STATEMENT THAT IS PRESENTED TO IT CONVINCINGLY. Then, having accepted this as the basis of its actions, it proceeds logically to do all in its power to bring it into being.

That is why the two most important words in the English language are the words . . "I AM." That is why the Ancients regarded these two words as the secret name of God.

You ask a friend how he is, and he replies carelessly . . "I am sick, I am poor, I am unlucky, I am subject to this, that or the other thing," . . never stopping to think that by those very words he is fastening misfortune upon himself, declaring to the subconscious mind within him that he IS sick or poor or weak or the servant of some desire.

"Let the weak say . . 'I AM strong!' " the Prophet Joel exhorted his people thousands of years ago. And the advice is as good today as it was then.

Robert Collier

As has been pointed out before, if some wise and omnipotent being were to live our lives for us, there would be no necessity for faith. This being could simply direct to the

Subconscious all those premises for good which would make our lives full and happy, and they would shortly come to pass. But the whole purpose of our lives is for us to provide the Subconscious with conclusions, premises, and knowledge of what we encounter in our specific areas; and what we forward as convictions the Subconscious returns to us in physical reality.

If the Subconscious Mind receives your conviction that you have money, you will have money. If it receives your conviction that you have health, you will have health. If it receives your conviction that you have love, you will have love. If it receives your conviction that you are successful, you will be successful. If it receives your conviction that you are wise, you will have wisdom. Whatever the premise, the Subconscious Mind will create it into physical reality. See how simple such a premise may be: "I have money," only that, and money is manifested. Why is it that we have such difficulty in doing this simple thing? It is because we lack faith! It is because the thing we want is expressed as hope, and in a million different ways throughout the day we affirm our faith in the very opposite!

Let us remember what Jesus said to those he healed: "You are well." He did not argue or postulate or advance pros and cons on the matter. He simply gave the Subconscious Mind a premise upon which it had to act by its very nature. What does the hypnotist do? He simply says, "You have no feeling in your arm," and the feeling immediately departs. It is upon such simple affirmations as these that the Subconscious Mind acts and always acts, and since we cannot think of anything without having certain convictions concerning it, the Subconscious Mind is always creating in our experience exactly what we believe in.

U.S. Andersen

Through the conscious mind we know ourselves as individuals, and take cognizance of the world about us. The subconscious mind is the storehouse of past thoughts.

We can understand the action of the conscious and subconscious minds by observing the process by which the child learns to play the piano. He is taught how to hold his hands and strike the keys, but at first he finds it somewhat difficult to control the movement of his fingers. He must practice daily, must concentrate his thoughts upon his fingers, consciously making the right movements.

These thoughts, in time, become subconscious, and the fingers are directed and controlled in the playing by the subconsciousness. In his first months, and possibly first years of practice, the pupil can perform only by keeping his conscious mind centered upon the work; but later he can play with ease and at the same time carry on a conversation with those about him, because the subconscious has become so thoroughly imbued with the idea of right movements that it can direct them without demanding the attention of the conscious mind.

The subconscious cannot take the initiative. It carried out only what is suggested by the conscious mind. But these suggestions it carries out faithfully, and it is this close relation between the conscious and subconscious which makes the conscious thinking so important.

Man's organism is controlled by the subconscious thought; circulation, breathing, digestion, and assimilation are all activities controlled by the subconscious. The subconscious is continually getting its impulses from the conscious, and we have only to change our conscious thought to get a corresponding change in the subconscious.

The Secrets, Mysteries & Powers of The Subconscious Mind

We live in a fathomless sea of plastic mind substance. This substance is ever alive and active. It is sensitive to the highest degree. It takes form according to the mental demand. Thought forms the mold or matrix from which the substance expresses. Our ideal is the mold from which our future will emerge.

The Universe is alive. In order to express life there must be mind; nothing can exist without mind. Everything which exists is some manifestation of this one basic substance from which and by which all things have been created and are continually being recreated. It is man's capacity to think that makes him a creator instead of a creature.

All things are the result of the thought process. Man has accomplished the seemingly impossible because he has refused to consider it impossible. By concentration men have made the connection between the finite and the Infinite, the limited and the Unlimited, the visible and the Invisible, the personal and the Impersonal.

Charles F. Haanel

Now where does the power of this Subconscious Mind cease? If you tell a sick man's Subconscious that he is well and he becomes well, if you tell an injured man's Subconscious that he feels no pain and he feels none, does this perhaps mean that you can tell an unsuccessful man that he is successful and he will become successful? It most certainly does.

Given the proper suggestion, the Subconscious Mind will manifest success from failure, health from disease, prosperity from poverty, friendship and love from loneliness and isolation. For nothing is impossible to the Subconscious Mind and it operates entirely by suggestion.

U.S. Andersen

The secret of being what you have it in you to be is simply this: Decide now what it is you want of life, exactly what you wish your future to be. Plan it out in detail. Vision it from start to finish. See yourself as you are now, doing those things you have always wanted to do. Make them REAL in your mind's eye . . feel them, live them, believe them, especially at the moment of going to sleep, when it is easiest to reach your subconscious mind . . and you will soon be seeing them in real life. It matters not whether you are young or old, rich or poor. The time to begin is NOW.

Do you want happiness? Do you want success? Do you want position, power, riches? Image them! How did God first make man? "In his image created He him." He "imaged" man in His Mind.

And that is the way everything has been made since time began. It was first imaged in Mind. That is the way everything you want must start . . with a mental image.

So use your imagination! Picture in it your Heart's Desire. Imagine it . . day-dream it so vividly, so clearly, that you will actually BELIEVE you HAVE it. In the moment that you carry this conviction to your subconscious mind . . in that moment your dream will become a reality. It may be a while before you realize it, but the important part is done. You have created the model. You can safely leave it to your subconscious mind to do the rest.

Robert Collier

Every normal human being is what he is, because of the decisions of his own will. Every normal human being has the power in himself to mold himself. The will of the conscious realm is absolute.

Millions of men are failures, because of the evil autosuggestions which they have permitted the conscious realms of their minds to give to the subconscious realms. Making any kind of suggestion to one's self, is autosuggestion.

If a man autosuggests to the subconscious realm of his mind, that he is a fool and a failure, how can he in the nature of things ever expect to be anything but a fool and a failure? Every such suggestion is accepted and believed by the subconscious realm; and it is what the subconscious realm believes, that is the standard of the man. A man actually is, what he makes the subconscious realm of his mind believe he is.

The subconscious realm is that part of a man's mind, which in the Bible is referred to as "The heart." "As he thinketh in his heart, so is he." This is not an opinion, but an inviolable law of God; an absolute statement of fact. The subconscious realm has power within itself to fashion the man according to its own beliefs.

The subconscious realm having neither reason nor judgment, has no means of knowing whether a statement made to it is reasonable or unreasonable, true or false, except through the reason and judgment of the conscious realm: and has no power to reject any suggestion, reasonable or unreasonable, true or false, except through the will of the conscious realm.

The functions of each realm are separate and distinct. The conscious realm is the seat of reason, judgment, will and the five senses; and these are not to be found in the subconscious or superconscious realms. The subconscious realm controls the circulation of the blood, digestion, respiration, involuntary muscular movements, and is the seat of intuition, memory, affection, emotion, conscience, belief, imagination, inspiration and genius; and these are not to be found in the conscious or superconscious realms.

For instance, the conscious realm can love only through the love of the subconscious realm; and the subconscious realm can will only through the will of the conscious realm. Each realm is dependent upon the other realms, for the functions of the other realms.

When men think only with the conscious realms, their thoughts are limited to the functions of the conscious realm; but when they expand their thinking to embrace the subconscious realms, their thought capacity is enlarged to the extent of the functions of the subconscious realm. Men have permitted the subconscious realms of their minds to lie practically dormant ever since the beginning of the human race; and the wonder is that they can be resuscitated.

Muscles of the body which are seldom used, become soft and flabby, and refuse to respond quickly even in time of need. The subconscious realm must be properly exercised and trained before it will respond satisfactorily. Being in a weakened condition by enforced idleness, it cannot be expected to respond powerfully under first instructions.

The subconscious realm is the great storehouse of the mind. In it is all the knowledge which has been gleaned through the years, by the study of the conscious realm. If properly directed and controlled, the subconscious realm can be made to give out all the knowledge which has been stored within it; at the time, and in the manner, that the will of the conscious realm may direct.

The memory, being one of the functions of the subconscious realm, is subject to control through suggestion and autosuggestion, and can be made to remember, or to cease to remember, at will. If the memory of some great grief, or disaster, or mistake, or sin, is constantly depressing one and interfering with the enjoyment of life, the subconscious realm can be instructed to cease to recall such an event; and it will obey the instruction.

" Forgetting those things which are behind, and reaching forth unto the things which are before, I press toward the mark for the prize of the high calling of God in Christ Jesus." It is also clear that the will of God exercises control over the function of memory in the mind of God, for He declares, "I will be merciful to their unrighteousness, and their sins and their iniquities will I remember no more."

Students who learn bow to control the subconscious realms of their minds, are delivered from nervousness and self-consciousness, which cause lack of memory at critical moments, such as examinations. If the conscious realm deposits treasures of thought in the subconscious realm, and then buries them under heaps of rubbish, it is not to be expected that they shall be found the instant they are wanted, at a time of crisis. It always takes time to find things, no matter how valuable they may be, if they have been carelessly stored away; and covered with a lot of trash. Treasures of thought, after they have been stored away, should be reviewed as frequently as possible.

The subconscious realm cannot give out more than has been stored within it. If the thought food, which the conscious realm has fed to the subconscious realm, has been trash, then the preponderance of the product of the subconscious realm will be trash. The subconscious realm has stored within it, all that it has received through the study of the conscious realm, through its own intuitions, through its contact with other minds, and through thought vibrations.

If it has been given opportunities to absorb wisdom through mingling with men of culture and education, it may have by absorption obtained enough intelligence to enable it to greatly improve upon the work of the conscious realm. If the subconscious realm has been starved through lack of good reading, or good thought food, it probably cannot be made to produce literature of real worth.

A man's library should be a striking index to his character. Most libraries need thinning out, like Gideon's army. God accomplished more with three hundred men of the right sort, than He could have accomplished with the original thirty two thousand men. Any student is better equipped with one dozen books of the right kind, than with a thousand books of the wrong kind.

Library shelves should not be filled with popular novels, but with books which abound in thoughts which a keen thinking man of spiritual discernment would be desirous of storing away in the subconscious realm of his mind for future helpfulness. A poorly written book impresses upon the subconscious realm, a poor style of writing; whereas a masterful book carries with it the impression of a masterful style of writing. One cannot afford to be careless even along one line. The influence of trashy reading cannot fail to manifest itself in one's work. The subconscious realm absorbs impressions continually.

The Secrets, Mysteries & Powers of The Subconscious Mind

The power of suggestion is so tremendous that it is impossible even to look upon a picture without being influenced to a considerable degree. The reading of the details of crime in one newspaper, effects one's thoughts detrimentally for weeks. There are so many thousands of worthy and helpful books, that it is almost criminal to waste precious time in reading trash. Subscribe only for good papers and read only helpful books.

Every thought, word, look and act of the conscious realm, has its influence upon the subconscious realm; and every such influence reacts upon the body, building it up or breaking it down, to that degree. Worry, anger, jealousy, malice, envy, bitterness, etc, act as poisons of a greater or lesser intensity, upon the organs of the body; and interfere with the functions of the same. Every good thought, or uplifting emotion, manufactures energy: whilst every evil thought, or degrading emotion, destroys energy.

Charles W. McCrossan

The Secrets, Mysteries & Powers of The Subconscious Mind

Christian Larson's "The Great Within"

(1907)

(Complete Book)

Table of Contents

Chapter 1 - Unlimited Possibilities
Chapter 2 - Desire and Faith
Chapter 3 - Impressing the Subconscious
Chapter 4 - Removing Wrong Impressions
Chapter 5 - Think on These Things
Chapter 6 - You Can Become What You Desire to Be
Chapter 7 - Developing the Genius Within
Chapter 8 - You May Become What You Wish to Be
Chapter 9 - Use of the Conscious and Subconscious
Chapter 10 - Solutions to Problems
Chapter 11 - Direct Assistance in Everything
Chapter 12 - Make Your Desires Subconscious
Chapter 13 - Produce Perfect Health
Chapter 14 - Impress the Subconscious Before Sleep
Chapter 15 - Sleeping on Difficult Problems
Chapter 16 - Sleep on the Superior; The Ideal
Chapter 17 - Awaking the Great Within

The Secrets, Mysteries & Powers of The Subconscious Mind
Christian Larson's "The Great Within"

Chapter 1

Unlimited Possibilities

THE mind of man is conscious and subconscious, objective and subjective, external and internal.

The conscious mind acts, the subconscious reacts; the conscious mind produces the impression, the subconscious produces the expression; the conscious mind determines what is to be done, the subconscious supplies the mental material and the necessary power. The subconscious mind is the great within . . an inner mental world from which all things proceed that appear in the being of man.

The conscious mind is the mind of action, the subconscious mind is the mind of reaction, but every subconscious reaction is invariably the direct result of a corresponding conscious action.

Every conscious action produces an impression upon the subconscious and every subconscious reaction produces an expression in the personality.

Everything that is expressed through the personality was first impressed upon the subconscious, and since the conscious mind may impress anything upon the subconscious, any desired expression may be secured, because the subconscious will invariably do what it is directed and impressed to do.

The subconscious mind is a rich mental field; every conscious impression is a seed sown in this field, and will bear fruit after its kind, be the seed good or otherwise.

The Secrets, Mysteries & Powers of The Subconscious Mind
Christian Larson's "The Great Within"

All thoughts of conviction and all deeply felt desires will impress themselves upon the subconscious and will reproduce their kind, to be later expressed in the personal being of man.

Every desire for power, ability, wisdom, harmony, joy, health, purity, life, greatness, will impress itself upon the subconscious, and will cause the thing desired to be produced in the great within, the quality and the quantity depending upon the depth of the desire and the conscious realization of the true idea conveyed by the desire.

What is produced in the within will invariably come forth into expression in the personality; therefore, by knowing how to impress the subconscious, man may give his personal self any quality desired, and in any quantity desired.

Personal power, physical health, mental brilliancy, remarkable ability, extraordinary talent, rare genius . . these are attainments that the subconscious of every mind can readily produce and bring forth when properly directed and impressed.

The subconscious mind obeys absolutely the desires of the conscious mind, and since the subconscious is limitless, it can do for man whatever he may desire to have done. What man may desire to become, that he can become, and the art of directing and impressing the subconscious is the secret.

Unlimited possibilities do exist in the subconscious of every mind, and since these possibilities can all be developed, there is no end to the attainments and achievements of man.

Nothing is impossible; the great within is limitless . . the inexhaustible source of everything that may be required for the highest development and the greatest accomplishments in human life, and whatever we may direct the within to produce, the same will invariably be produced.

Chapter 2

Desire and Faith

TO properly direct and impress the subconscious, the first essential is to realize that the subconscious mind is a finer mentality that permeates every fiber of the entire personality. Though the subconscious can be impressed most directly through the brain-center, the volume of subconscious expression will increase in proportion to our conscious realization of subconscious life in every part of mind and body.

To concentrate attention frequently upon the subconscious side of the entire personality will steadily awaken the great within; this will cause one to feel that a new and superior being is beginning to unfold, and with that feeling comes the conviction that unbounded power does exist in the deeper life of man.

When the awakening of the subconscious is felt in every part of mind and body, one knows that anything may be attained and achieved; doubts disappear absolutely, because to feel the limitless is to believe in the limitless.

While impressing the subconscious, attention should be directed upon the inside of mind, and this is readily done while one thinks that the subconscious mentality permeates the personality, as water permeates a sponge.

Think of the interior essence that permeates the exterior substance, and cause all mental actions to move toward the finer mental life that lives and moves and has its being within the interior mind. This will cause the conscious action to impress itself directly upon the subconscious, and a corresponding reaction or expression will invariably follow.

While directing attention upon the subconscious, the idea that is to be impressed should be clearly discerned in mind and an effort should be made to feel the soul of that idea.

To mentally feel the soul of the idea will completely eliminate the mechanical tendency of mental action, and this is extremely important because no mechanical action of mind can impress the subconscious.

Perfect faith in the process is indispensable, and to inwardly know that results will be secured is to cause failure to become impossible.

The deeper and higher the attitude of faith while the subconscious is being impressed, the more deeply will the impression be made, and the deep impression not only enters the richest states of the subconscious, but always produces results.

The attitude of faith takes the mind into the superior, the limitless, the soul of things, and this is precisely what is wanted.

When the mind transcends the objective it enters into the subjective, and to enter into the subjective is to impress one's ideas and desires directly, deeply and completely upon the great within. Such impressions will invariably produce remarkable expressions, not only because they have entered more deeply into the subconscious, but also because every impression that is made in the attitude of faith is given superior quality, greater power and higher worth.

The Secrets, Mysteries & Powers of The Subconscious Mind
Christian Larson's "The Great Within"

The subconscious should never be approached in the attitude of command or demand, but always in the attitude of faith and desire. Never command the subconscious to do thus or so, but desire with a deep, strong desire, that the subconscious do what you desire to have done, and animate that desire with the faith that it positively will be done.

To combine a high faith with a strong desire while impressing the subconscious is the secret through which results may invariably be secured.

The subconscious should never be forcefully aroused, but should be gradually awakened and developed through such actions of mind as are deep and strong while perfectly serene.

Deep thoughts on all important subjects, lofty aspirations on all occasions, and a constantly expanding consciousness will aid remarkably in awakening the great within.

Whenever attention is directed upon the subconscious, an effort should be made to expand consciousness by picturing upon mind the expanding process while the deeper feeling of thought is placing itself in touch with the universal; a strong, deep desire for greater things should be impressed upon the inner mentality, and a deep stillness should animate every action of mind.

The inner side of mind should always be acted upon peacefully, though not with that peacefulness that has a tendency to produce inaction, but with that peacefulness that produces a high, strong action that continues to act in serenity and poise.

To concentrate a strong, deeply felt, well poised mental action upon the entire subconscious mentality a number of times every day will, in a remarkably short time, develop the great within to such an extent that the mind will inwardly know that unlimited power and innumerable possibilities have been placed at its command, and when this realization comes the mind may go on to any attainment and any achievement; failure will be simply impossible.

When the development of the subconscious has been promoted to a degree the conscious mind will instinctively feel that failure is impossible, and will, consequently, leave results to the law. There will be no anxiety about results because to feel the presence of subconscious action is to know that results must follow when the subconscious is properly directed and impressed.

Perfect faith in the law that the subconscious will invariably do whatever it is impressed to do will eliminate anxiety completely, and this is extremely important, because the subconscious mind cannot proceed to do what it has been impressed to do so long as there is anxiety in the conscious mind.

Provide the proper conditions and the law will positively produce the desired results, and to inwardly know this is the first essential in providing the proper conditions.

The subconscious mind is somewhat similar to the phonograph; under certain conditions it can record anything, and under certain other conditions it can reproduce everything that has been recorded. There is this difference, however: The subconscious not only reproduces exactly what has been recorded, but will also form, create, develop and express what mind may desire when the impression is being made; that is, the subconscious not only reproduces the seed itself, but as many more seeds as the original seed desired to reproduce, and also the exact degree of improvement in quality that was latent in the desire of the original seed or impression.

The subconscious not only reproduces the mental idea contained in the impression, but also every essential that may be required to fulfill the desire of that impression.

Through this law the subconscious can find the answer to any question or work out any problem when properly impressed with an exact idea of what is wanted.

Chapter 3

Impressing the Subconscious

THE subconscious provides the essentials, but the conscious mind must apply those essentials before practical results may be secured.

When the subconscious is directed to produce health, those mental actions will be expressed that can produce health in the body when combined with normal physical actions, and it is the conscious mind that must produce the normal physical actions; that is, common sense living. When the subconscious is directed to produce success, those elements, qualities and powers will be expressed in mind and body that can, if consciously applied, produce success.

That the subconscious can do anything is absolutely true, but it is true in this sense, that it can supply the power, the capacity and the understanding to do anything, but the conscious mind must practically apply what the subconscious has brought forth into expression.

The subconscious supplies the power and the mental elements, but these must be used by the conscious mind if the desired results are to be secured. Nothing comes ready-made from the subconscious, but it can give us the material from which we can make anything.

The subconscious can give you the powers and qualities of genius, and if you apply, practically and constantly, those powers and qualities, you will become a genius. The subconscious can give you the life and the power that is necessary to remarkable talents, and if you use that life and

The Secrets, Mysteries & Powers of The Subconscious Mind
Christian Larson's "The Great Within"

power in the daily cultivation of your talents, those talents will become remarkable.

The law is that the conscious mind must impress its desires upon the subconscious in order to secure the mental essentials that may be required to fulfill those desires, but the conscious mind must use those essentials before results can be secured.

It is the conscious mind that does things, but it is the subconscious that supplies the power with which those things are done, and by learning to draw upon the subconscious the conscious mind can do anything, because unbounded power and innumerable possibilities are latent in the great within.

The proper conditions for recording an impression upon the subconscious are deep feeling, strong desires, conscious interest and a living faith. When these are blended harmoniously in the conscious actions of mind the subconscious will be directed and impressed properly and the desired response will invariably appear.

The principal essential, however, is deep feeling; no idea or desire can enter the subconscious unless it is deeply felt, and every idea or desire that is deeply felt will enter the subconscious of itself, whether or not we desire to have it do so. It is through this law that man is affected by his environments, surroundings and external conditions, because whenever he permits himself to be deeply impressed by that with which he may come in contact those impressions will enter the subconscious.

What enters the subconscious of any mind will become a part of that mind, and will, to a degree, affect the nature, the character, the quality, the thoughts and the actions of that mind. When the subconscious is impressed by external conditions the impressions will be like those conditions and, as like produces like, conditions will be produced in the subconscious that are exactly like those external conditions from which the impressions came.

The individual, therefore, who permits his subconscious to be indiscriminately impressed by external conditions will think and act, more or less, as his environments may suggest. In many respects his life will be controlled completely by those persons and things with which he may come in contact, while in nearly all other respects his life will be greatly modified by the presence of those persons and things.

The mind that does not control its feelings may be subconsciously impressed by any external action, be that action good or otherwise, while the mind that can give deep feeling to any idea can impress any idea upon the subconscious, and as the whole of the individual life is determined by what the subconscious is directed or impressed to do, the former will become, more or less, like his environment, having control neither of himself nor his destiny; the latter, however, may become what he wants to become and will master both himself and his destiny.

No undesirable feeling should ever be permitted; no wrong idea should ever be given in thought; nor should one ever think seriously, feelingly or sympathetically about wrong or evil in any shape or form.

To think feelingly about wrong is to impress wrong upon the subconscious; it is to sow undesirable seeds in the garden of the mind, and a harvest of weeds . . sickness, trouble and want, will be the result.

The Secrets, Mysteries & Powers of The Subconscious Mind
Christian Larson's "The Great Within"

Good thoughts, deeply felt, will bring health, happiness, harmony, peace, power, ability and character. Wrong thoughts, deeply felt, will bring discord, depression, fear, sickness, weakness and failure.

To properly impress the subconscious at all times, it is therefore necessary to train the mind to think only of those things that one desires to realize and express in tangible life; and what one does not wish to meet in personal experience should never be given a single moment of thought.

What we mentally feel we invariably impress upon the subconscious, and there is a tendency to mentally feel every thought that is given prolonged or serious attention.

To think about that which we do not want, is to impress upon the subconscious what we do not wish to impress; and as every impression produces a corresponding expression, we will thereby receive the very things we desire to avoid.

It is through this law that what we fear always comes upon us, because what we fear will impress itself upon the subconscious without fail.

To fear disease, failure or trouble is to sow seeds in the subconscious field that will bring forth a harvest of diseased conditions, troubled thoughts, confused mental states and misdirected actions in mind and body.

The more intense the fear the deeper the subconscious impression, and the more we shall receive of that which we feared we should receive.

Through the same law we always receive what we continue to expect in the desire of the deep, strong faith. The more faith we have in the realization and attainment of that which has quality, superiority and worth, the more deeply we impress the subconscious with those mental seeds that can and will bring forth the greater good that we desire.

To have faith in the attainment of peace, harmony, health, power, ability, talent and genius, while directing the subconscious to produce those things, is to cause those very things to be created within us in greater and greater measure.

Chapter 4

Removing Wrong Impressions

THE purpose of consciously and intelligently directing the subconscious is first, to correct every wrong, every flaw, every defect, every perversion, and every imperfect condition that may exist in the personality of man; and, second, to bring out into fuller expression the limitless possibilities that exist in the great within.

Everything that is wrong in the personal life of the individual comes from a corresponding wrong impression in the subconscious; the wrong subconscious impression is the cause, the wrong external condition is the effect; it is therefore evident that to remove all wrong impressions from the subconscious is to establish complete emancipation throughout the entire personal being of man.

To remove any wrong impression from the subconscious, the opposite correct impression must be made in its place. A wrong impression cannot be removed by mental force, resistance or denial; produce the right impression and the wrong impression will cease to exist.

By training the mind to think only of that which is desired in actual realization and experience, and by deeply impressing all those thoughts and desires upon the subconscious, every undesirable impression will be removed; the cause of every flaw, defect or perversion in the personal man will be removed, and in consequence, the flaws, defects, and perversions themselves will cease to exist.

The entire subconscious field can be changed absolutely by constantly causing new and superior impressions to be

The Secrets, Mysteries & Powers of The Subconscious Mind
Christian Larson's "The Great Within"

formed in the great within; and every change that is brought about in the subconscious will produce a corresponding change in mind and body.

There is nothing adverse in the mentality or the personality of man that cannot be corrected by causing the correct impression to be formed in the subconscious. All wrongs, flaws or defects, whether they be hereditary, or personally produced, can be removed completely through the intelligent direction of the subconscious.

Every impression that is properly made in the subconscious mind will produce a corresponding expression in the personality; that is the law, and it cannot fail; but the impression must be properly made.

The subconscious does not respond to mere commands, because it neither reasons nor discriminates; it does not obey what it is told to do, but what it is impressed to do. It is the idea that enters into the subconscious that determines subconscious action; but the idea must not simply be given to the subconscious, it must enter into the subconscious.

The idea that predominates in mind while the subconscious is being directed, is the idea that will be impressed; therefore, negative desires will impress the subconscious to do the very opposite to what is desired by the desire.

To direct the subconscious to remove sickness is to impress the idea of sickness, because the mind thinks principally of sickness at the time; in consequence, more sickness will be produced.

It is not what the subconscious is directed to do, but the predominant thought that is conveyed through that direction that determines results; therefore, the predominant thought must be identical with the final results desired.

When health is desired, no thought whatever should be given to sickness; the subconscious should not be directed to remove sickness, but should be directed to produce health.

The subconscious should always be directed to produce those qualities and conditions that are desired, but those conditions that are to be removed should never be mentioned in mind. Adverse conditions will disappear of themselves When true conditions are established; but the mind cannot impress, create and establish the true while attention is being concentrated upon the adverse.

To direct the subconscious not to do thus or so, is to impress the subconscious to do that very thing. When you try to impress the subconscious with the idea that you do not wish to get sick any more you have sickness in mind, and it is the idea that you have in mind that you impress upon the subconscious. To remove sickness forget sickness absolutely, and impress upon the subconscious the idea of health, and that idea alone. Desire health with all the power of mind, and fill both sides of mentality, conscious and subconscious, so completely with that desire that every thought of sickness is forgotten.

A denial will impress upon the subconscious the nature and the power of the very thing that is denied; therefore, to deny evil or resist evil is to produce causes in mind that will, in the coming days, produce more evil.

To try to deny away adverse conditions is to continue in perpetual mental warfare with those very things that mind is trying to destroy. Temporary states of seeming freedom in some parts of the system will be followed regularly with outbreaks of adversity in other parts; while the subconscious cause of undesirable conditions in mind or body will not be removed.

So long as we continue to resist or deny evil, we will think about evil, and so long as we think about evil, evil will be impressed upon the subconscious; and whatever we impress upon the subconscious, that the subconscious will reproduce and bring forth into the personal life. When we have a great undertaking that we wish to promote, and desire to secure as much added power, ability and capacity as possible from the great within, the subconscious should not be directed to prevent failure. To think of failure is to impress the subconscious with the idea of failure, and detrimental conditions . . conditions that will confuse the mind and produce failure . . will be expressed.

All thought of failure should be eliminated, and the subconscious should be deeply impressed to produce success. The subconscious will respond by bringing forth the power, the capacity, the ability, the understanding and the determination that can and will produce success.

The Secrets, Mysteries & Powers of The Subconscious Mind
Christian Larson's "The Great Within"

Chapter 5

Think on These Things

WHEN properly directed, the subconscious mind can inspire the conscious mind to do the right thing at the right time, to take advantage of opportunities during the psychological moment, and to so deal with circumstances that all things will work together to promote the object in view. It is, therefore, evident that when the subconscious is trained to work in harmony with the objects and desires of the conscious mind, failure becomes impossible, and success in greater and greater measures may be secured by anyone.

When trying to remove undesirable habits, tendencies or desires, the mind should never think, "I shall not do this anymore," because through such a thought or statement, the habit in mind will be re-impressed upon the subconscious and will gain a deeper foothold in the system than it had before.

The proper course to pursue is to forget completely what you desire to remove; refuse to think of it; when tempted to think of the matter turn attention upon the opposite qualities, desires or tendencies. Should you fail to become sufficiently interested in those opposite desires to forget what you want to forget, look for the most interesting points of view connected with those desires. The mental effort employed in trying to find the most interesting point of view connected with those desires will cause the mind to become thoroughly interested in those desires, and will, consequently, forget those things that should be forgotten.

The Secrets, Mysteries & Powers of The Subconscious Mind
Christian Larson's "The Great Within"

When the mind is being interested in those desires that you wish to cultivate, they should be impressed upon the subconscious with all the depth of feeling that can possibly be aroused. These impressions should be repeated a number of times every day, and the new desires will soon take root in the subconscious.

Every desire or tendency that takes root in the subconscious will begin to develop and express itself in the personal self, and will be felt throughout the personality. When the new desire is fully expressed, it will be thoroughly felt; and since no two desires of opposite nature can exist in the person at the same time, the old desires will disappear; the old tendencies and the old habits will have vanished completely.

To impress upon the subconscious a strong desire for the better, the purer and the superior, is to cause the system to crave something better; the force of desire will be refined; the entire organism will be purified, and the wants of the personal self will become normal on a higher plane.

All kinds of undesirable habits may be removed by constantly impressing upon the subconscious the idea of pure desire; and all tendencies to anger, hatred and similar states, may be removed by causing the qualities of love, kindness, justice and sympathy to be more fully developed in the great within.

To remove fear and worry, impress the subconscious, as frequently as possible, with the deep feeling of faith, gratitude and mental sunshine.

To have faith is to know that man has the power to perpetually increase the good, and that he may constantly press on to better things and greater things. To have faith is to be guided by superior mental lucidity, and thereby know how to select what is safe and secure; and he who knows that he is on the safe path, the ascending path, the endless path to better things and greater things, has eliminated fear absolutely.

To live constantly in the spirit of gratitude is not only to remove worry, but the cause of worry. To be grateful for the good that is now coming into life is to open the way for the coming of greater good. This is the law; and he who is daily receiving the greater good, has no cause for' worry; he will even forget that worry ever had a place in his mind. To constantly impress the subconscious with mental sunshine, is to establish the tendency to live on the bright side, the sunny side; and to live on the bright side is to increase your own brightness; your mind will become more brilliant, your thinking will have more lucidity and clearness, your nature will have more sweetness, your personality will be in more perfect harmony with everything, your life will be better, your work will be better . . everything will be better; therefore, by living on the bright side, all things will steadily become better and brighter for you.

When all is dark, and everything seems to go wrong, arouse all your energies for the purpose of impressing and directing the subconscious to produce the change you desire. Give the deepest possible feeling to those impressions, and have stronger faith than you ever had before.

Continue persistently until the great within begins to respond; you will then feel from within how to act, and you will be given the power to do what you feel you should do. Ere long, things will take a turn; the threatened calamity will be avoided by the coming forth of that power within, that is greater than all adversities, all troubles, all wrongs; and

The Secrets, Mysteries & Powers of The Subconscious Mind
Christian Larson's "The Great Within"

instead, this power, having been awakened, will proceed to create a better future than you ever knew before."

Chapter 6

You Can Become What You Desire to Be...

WHILE the subconscious is being impressed, no thought whatever should be given to limitation, and no comparisons should be made with other persons or previous attainments. To think that you wish to do better today than you did yesterday, is to give the subconscious two unrelated ideas upon which to act . . the idea of the lesser achievement of the past and the idea of the greater achievement of the future. The subconscious will try to reproduce them both, but as they are antagonistic, they will neutralize each other, and there will be no results. The greater and the lesser cannot be produced by the same force at the same tune. To impress the desire that you may become greater than anyone else, will also present to the subconscious two conflicting ideas; and the results again will be neutralized.

The course to pursue is to forget the lesser achievements of yesterday; think only of the greater achievements that you wish to promote today; then direct the subconscious to do today what you wish to have done today. This will cause the great within to give all its power and attention to the one idea . . the greater achievement of today; and the greater achievement will positively follow. Know what you desire to become; resolve to become what you desire to become, whether others have reached those heights or not; forget the lesser heights that others have reached and give your whole mind and soul to the greater heights that you have resolved to reach.

You can become what you desire to become; the great within is limitless, and can give you all the wisdom and all

The Secrets, Mysteries & Powers of The Subconscious Mind
Christian Larson's "The Great Within"

the power that you may require. Knowing this, direct the great within to bring forth what you may need to reach your lofty goal, and the same will be done. The subconscious never fails to do what it is properly directed to do.

While impressing the subconscious, think of the perfect in regard to quality, and the limitless in regard to quantity. Never specify any exact amount, nor any special degree; always desire the limitless and the perfect; desire nothing less; and animate consciousness with a strong desire to expand constantly during the process, so that the highest quality and the greatest quantity possible may be realized.

Desire the fullest possible expression in the great eternal now; realize that your own inherent powers and capabilities are limitless, and impress that idea upon the subconscious.

Give no thought whatever to the lesser attainments in your own life or in the lives of others, but keep your mental eye single upon what you wish to become, knowing that you can become what you wish to become because there are no limitations in the great within.

When the subconscious begins to respond, a distinct sensation is frequently felt of some interior power working through you; this means that greater power from within is being awakened, and the outer mind should give full right of way so that a complete expression may be secured; that is, the conscious mind should become quiet, serene and thoroughly receptive, and should forget the personal self, for the time.

When the personal self is forgotten and the greater interior self is given full possession of both the mentality and the personality . . it is then that one's greatest work is done.

The Secrets, Mysteries & Powers of The Subconscious Mind
Christian Larson's "The Great Within"

It is then that real ability, real talent and real genius can appear in tangible life and action.

When the musician forgets herself, there is something in her music that awakens the very depths of the soul, and you are lifted to a faker world than you ever knew before.

When the artist forgets himself, his pictures are given immortal life and every touch reveals a universe of indescribable beauty.

When the orator forgets himself, he speaks as one having authority, and you inwardly feel that every word is true.

When the practical man of affairs forgets himself, he is given a power that is irresistible, and the obstacles that are encountered in the way, disappear as if they never had the slightest existence.

It is such people that do great things in the world; it is such people who live in the human heart after ages have passed away; and their secret is this . . the greatness within them was awakened, and was permitted to give full expression to its rare and superior power.

When you feel this higher power mysteriously moving within the greater depths of mind and soul, you know what is taking place; be calm, and give the superior self the right of way. At first this power may feel as if it were distinct from yourself; but it is not, it is your own superior power; the coming forth of your own limitless power; the very power that you have for some time been directing the subconscious to produce; and when you feel that it is your own it is placed in your full conscious possession, and will do whatever you may desire or direct.

The Secrets, Mysteries & Powers of The Subconscious Mind
Christian Larson's "The Great Within"

To inwardly feel that the entire within is your own is extremely important, because the more completely the conscious mind is united with the power of the subconscious, the more perfectly can the conscious mind impress the subconscious, and the more thoroughly can the greater power of the subconscious express itself in external, tangible action.

When you are about to do something that demands the best that is within you, impress the subconscious for higher power; then wait a few moments for this power to appear; and when it does appear, let the outer self obey. The great within has come forth to do your work, and no power in existence can do it better.

To enter into full conscious possession of the higher power from within, and to give full right of way to this power, is to give your objective talents and faculties the greatest power and the best power at your command.

The Secrets, Mysteries & Powers of The Subconscious Mind
Christian Larson's "The Great Within"

Chapter 7

Developing the Genius Within

TO impress the subconscious for more power it is necessary to give to that impression all the power that mind is conscious of now; in other words, the seed that is already at hand should be placed in rich soil; the power that is now active in the conscious mind should be caused to act upon the subconscious; there will be increase; and by re-impressing the added power upon the subconscious every time added power is gained, this increase will become perpetual.

To proceed, concentrate attention upon the subconscious side of the entire personality, and desire gently, but with deep feeling, to draw all the present active energies of the system into the subconscious.

The more energy that is drawn into the subconscious during this process, the more power will be impressed upon the subconscious, and the more power that is impressed upon the subconscious the more power will be expressed from the subconscious.

The law is that whatever power is impressed upon the subconscious will return to the outer personality with added power, just as every seed sown in rich soil will reproduce itself, ten, twenty, sixty and even a hundredfold.

Therefore, to daily arouse all the power that we personally possess, and to impress all of that power upon the subconscious, is to increase perpetually the quantity of personal power; and the quality of that power can be steadily improved by transmuting and refining all the present forces of the system before they are impressed upon the subconscious.

Before the conscious mind begins to act upon the subconscious all thought and all feeling should be elevated into the highest states of quality, worth and superiority that can possibly be realized. This will cause the impression to be superior, and a superior impression will produce a superior expression.

That which is common, ordinary or inferior should never be held in mind, nor deeply felt for a moment, because to feel the ordinary is to impress the ordinary upon the subconscious; it is sowing inferior seed, and the harvest will be cheap, common, worthless.

No person should ever think of himself as inferior, or permit himself to recognize the imperfect in his nature. To recognize or feel the imperfect is to sow more seeds of imperfection, and reap another harvest that is not worthwhile.

There is a superior nature within man; this nature alone should be recognized and felt; only those thoughts and ideas that are formed in the exact likeness of the superior should be impressed upon the subconscious, and the subconscious will respond by giving superiority to the entire mentality and the entire personality.

The average person fails to improve because he lives mainly in the consciousness of his imperfections; he feels that he is ordinary and constantly impresses the subconscious with this feeling of the ordinary; the subconscious naturally responds by producing the ordinary, both in mind and body.

The Secrets, Mysteries & Powers of The Subconscious Mind
Christian Larson's "The Great Within"

That person, however, who lives in the ideal, who thinks constantly of the greater worth that is within him, and who tries to feel and realize his superior nature, will give quality to every impression that may enter the subconscious; and according to the law of action and reaction, will steadily develop greater quality and worth throughout his entire nature.

The quality of the impression that is given to the subconscious always corresponds with the degree of quality of which we are conscious at the tune the impression is made. To refine, elevate and enrich all thought and feeling before the conscious mind begins to act upon the subconscious, is therefore of the highest importance.

The more quality that is given to the power that is being developed, the greater the results that may be secured through the application of that power.

It is quality and quantity combined that produces greatness, and greatness . . greater and greater greatness, is the purpose we all have in view.

To constantly feel the greatness of the great within, is to constantly impress upon the subconscious the idea of greatness; this will cause the subconscious to develop greatness and express greatness through every part of the personal man.

As greatness develops, the feeling of greatness will become deeper, stronger and more intense; this will cause larger and finer ideas of greatness to be impressed upon the subconscious; and the result of these later impressions will be larger and greater expressions; a larger measure of greatness will be developed perpetually through the law of much gathering more, or "to him that hath shall be given."

The Secrets, Mysteries & Powers of The Subconscious Mind
Christian Larson's "The Great Within"

All development comes from the subconscious, and since the possibilities of the great within are limitless, anyone can, through the proper direction of the subconscious, develop remarkable ability, extraordinary talent and rare genius.

All genius is the result of a large subconscious mentality therefore, anyone can become a genius by awakening a larger and a larger measure of the great within.

That a genius is asleep in the subconscious of every mind is literally true, but to awaken this genius is not the only essential; the conscious mind must be cultivated scientifically, so that the superior ability from within may find free and full expression.

The conscious mind should be cultivated, the subconscious should be developed; the conscious mind should be trained to do things, while the subconscious should be directed to give more and more power for the doing of greater and greater things.

The subconscious has the capacity to produce genius in any mind . . the greatest genius imaginable, but the conscious mind must be highly cultivated so as to become a fit instrument through which great genius may find expression for its superior work.

When quality and worth are received from the subconscious, the conscious mind should use those things in practical action, so that the outer elements and forces of mind may be trained to appreciate quality and appropriate worth in all their tangible expressions.

The conscious and the subconscious sides of mind should be placed in the most perfect harmonious relations, so that every impression of the conscious mind may enter

The Secrets, Mysteries & Powers of The Subconscious Mind
Christian Larson's "The Great Within"

deeply into the subconscious and every expression from the subconscious may work through the conscious mind without any restriction or interference whatever.

The entire mind develops through the attainment of deeper and higher states of consciousness of the great within; and as this interior realm is boundless, there is no end to the possibilities of mental development.

To gain this ulterior consciousness, objective consciousness should be constantly deepened toward the unfathomable within, and this is accomplished by training all the mental tendencies to move toward the within.

The mental tendencies will move toward those states of being to which we give the greatest amount of attention; therefore, by constantly thinking with deep feeling of the great within, all the mental tendencies will move toward, and into, the great within; and will carry into the subconscious every idea, thought or desire that the conscious mind may wish to realize and fulfill.

When all the mental tendencies move into the subconscious, and all thought is given feeling, worth and quality, the subconscious will constantly be impressed with superior ideas, which means a constant expression of superior life, superior ability and superior power.

The more deeply the tendencies of mind enter the subconscious, the more of the great within will be awakened; and whatever is awakened in the within will invariably come forth into the personal man.

It is therefore evident that when we cease to live on the surface of personal life we shall constantly improve that surface; by mentally living in the within we shall strengthen,

The Secrets, Mysteries & Powers of The Subconscious Mind
Christian Larson's "The Great Within"

enrich and perfect the without; that is, we improve external effects by going more deeply into the subconscious and increasing the quality and the power of internal causes.

The person who actually enters the deeper life to live will not ignore the body; those who simply dream of inner states of life may neglect the body, but those who thoroughly develop the greater, inner life will become able to give the body the best that can be secured; and they will enjoy physical existence infinitely more than those who simply live on the surface. It is the truth that whatever we awaken and develop in the great within will invariably come forth into tangible, personal expression.

Chapter 8

You May Become What You Wish to Be

EACH person is, no more and no less, than what has been given to him by his subconscious mind; and as the subconscious is prepared to give as much as anyone may desire, the statement that we all may become whatsoever we may wish to become, is therefore absolutely true; but what the subconscious is to give to any person depends largely upon the movement of his mental tendencies.

All the creative energies of the system follow the tendencies of the mind; therefore, when all the mental tendencies move toward the subconscious, all the surplus energy that is generated in the system will enter the subconscious; and the more energy that enters the subconscious the more of the subconscious will be awakened and developed.

The larger the field that is placed under cultivation the greater the harvest.

Every mental tendency that is trained to enter the subconscious will cause a corresponding tendency to be permanently expressed; therefore, by causing all the worthy tendencies to move toward the subconscious, the subconscious will respond by expressing through the personality the tendencies to be just, true, honest, virtuous, kind, sympathetic, sweet-tempered, cheerful, fearless, faithful, persevering, industrious . . in brief, everything that goes to make a strong and worthy personality.

The Secrets, Mysteries & Powers of The Subconscious Mind
Christian Larson's "The Great Within"

By a simple system of subconscious training, anyone can build up the strongest and most beautiful character imaginable, and in a reasonable time make it a permanent part of himself. A lack of character is due wholly to the fact that the subconscious has been improperly impressed; misleading tendencies have been formed, and let it be remembered that nothing can tempt man to go wrong except the perverse tendencies that are expressed from his own subconscious mind.

Every weak place in mind or character is caused by a subconscious tendency that is going wrong; such tendencies may have been inherited . . many of them are, but they can all be corrected by daily directing the subconscious to produce the opposite quality.

To think, with conviction, that human, nature is weak, is to impress upon the subconscious the idea of weakness, and the subconscious will respond by producing a tendency to weakness. Therefore, he who thinks he is weak will cause his nature to continue to be weak. We are weak or strong according to what we direct the subconscious to produce in us.

To realize that the great within contains the power to make the personality as strong as we may wish it to be, and to impress upon the subconscious a strong desire for that power, is to direct the subconscious to make us strong; and whatever we direct the subconscious to do, the same will invariably be done.

There is no reason whatever why any person should continue to have a weak body, a weak character or a weak mind; anything in the being of man can be made strong if the subconscious is properly directed to bring forth the greater life and the greater power.

The Secrets, Mysteries & Powers of The Subconscious Mind
Christian Larson's "The Great Within"

When the great within is awakened we have the powerful personality, the giant mind, the irresistible character and the great soul. The natural result is a great life . . a life that is too strong to be tempted, too strong to be swayed or disturbed by adversity, too strong to be turned from the path to its lofty goal. Such a life will not only live a life that is life, but will be an endless inspiration to the race; and such a life is waiting in the great within of every soul.

Chapter 9

Use of the Conscious and Subconscious

THE great within is the source of inspirations, all real music, all permanent art, all poetry with soul, all rich thought, all ideas of genuine worth, all invention, all discovery, all science, and the truth that is absolute.

Everything that has worth, be it in a small degree, or in a very great degree, comes directly from the richness of the subconscious; therefore, to do the greater, the mind should enter into the closest touch with the great within, and should expect the very best that the limitless within can produce.

When in need of ideas, plans, methods, ways and means, call upon the subconscious; the call will not be in vain; the subconscious can supply every need, and will invariably do so when properly directed.

While directing the subconscious, however, all conscious action must be in absolute poise; it is not only necessary to impress what we desire but to impress that desire in such a way that it will actually produce an impression.

When in the presence of the great fact that the within is limitless, the mind will naturally become enthusiastic; feeling will run high and is very liable to become overwrought; but such a feeling has no depth, it is simply superficial emotionalism; it will waste any amount of energy, but will never produce a single impression upon the subconscious.

To impress the subconscious, the mind must be calm, the entire personality must be in poise, and this feeling of poise must have that great depth that touches the very soul of life itself.

Not the slightest trace of emotional enthusiasm must be permitted, nor must feeling run toward the surface at any time; the actions of mind, especially those of feeling, must move toward the great within if the subconscious is to be reached.

There must be no anxiety connected with the desire to impress the subconscious, and every form of doubt must be eliminated completely.

To properly impress the subconscious, faithful application is necessary; also constant practice, and a perseverance that will not give up; but the prize is worthy of the effort. To realize that the subconscious can, and will, do anything when properly impressed, is to persevere until the proper impression has been made; and it is those who work in this realization that secure the marvelous results.

To eliminate the tendency to feel emotional while acting upon the subconscious, cultivate the substantial feeling; train yourself to feel substantial at all times, and wild, empty, overwrought feelings will entirely disappear.

It is the proper feeling that determines the proper impression; the attainment of the deep, substantial feeling is therefore extremely important, though it is equally important to be able to feel the vibrations of the finer forces of the system.

It is the finer forces that impress the subconscious and the subconscious is invariably impressed whenever these forces are felt.

The Secrets, Mysteries & Powers of The Subconscious Mind
Christian Larson's "The Great Within"

To develop the consciousness of the finer forces, attention should be frequently concentrated upon that life that permeates the tangible elements in every part of being; and during this concentration the feeling of consciousness should be deepened and expanded as much as possible.

Every conscious action should be trained to penetrate to the very depth of life, and during this process the mind should act in the realization that the more deeply it penetrates any element in the personality, the finer will be the forces into which consciousness will enter.

To awaken or arouse any force or element, attention should be concentrated upon that state in which the desired force or element is known to exist, and the mind should think of the nature of that force or element according to the best possible understanding that can be formed of that nature.

The same method may be employed in the development of the subconscious side of any desired faculty or talent.

The creative energies of the system always build up those qualities of which the mind may be thinking; therefore, to actually and continually think of the real nature of a great talent is to develop that talent into the same degree of greatness that is discerned in mind.

The power of this method in the development of ability, talent and genius is practically unlimited, because the mind is capable of discerning higher and higher degrees of greatness, and the subconscious is capable of providing creative energies of as high a state of fineness and power as may be required.

The Secrets, Mysteries & Powers of The Subconscious Mind
Christian Larson's "The Great Within"

To secure the best results from any method through which the great within is to be unfolded and expressed, it is extremely important to use properly the conscious and the subconscious factors of mind at the various stages of the process.

While impressing the subconscious, the conscious mind should be strong, firm, positive and highly active, but should become perfectly quiet and receptive while expecting a response from the subconscious.

Harmony, serenity and poise are indispensable states both when the impression is being made and when the expression is expected.

The right use of the will is of extraordinary importance; and neither time nor effort should be spared in establishing this right use, because where the will is misapplied the subconscious expressions are interfered with to such an extent that results are completely neutralized. While the subconscious is being impressed, the will should act firmly and directly upon that consciousness that is felt in the subconscious, but when the subconscious is expected to respond the will should be relaxed into a state of complete inaction.

It is not the purpose of the will to control the outer person by acting directly upon the outer person; the will controls the outer person by causing the subconscious to produce in the outer person whatever may be desired; but when the subconscious begins to express what the will has desired and directed, the will must, for the time being, cease to act.

The true function of the will is to act upon the finer states of consciousness; that is, the subconscious states, those states that are felt in the deeper life of the personality or the mentality; and while in such action, to impress upon the subconscious those causes that can produce the desired effects.

When these causes have been impressed, and the time has come for the expected results, the will must withdraw so that the personality may become sufficiently receptive to give the subconscious response the fullest and freest possible expression.

The subconscious expression will come of itself, at the tune designated, if the impression has been properly made; but every attempt of the will to help draw forth that expression will interfere with results.

When the desired subconscious expression fails to appear at the time designated, the impression has either not been properly made, or the subconscious response is being prevented by too much active will force, anxiety or objective commotion.

The subconscious cannot express itself, or do what it is directed to do unless the outer mentality and personality are in poise; but perfect poise is not possible so long as will power is applied upon the external side of mind or body.

Train the will to act upon the subconscious, and the subconscious only, and this is readily accomplished by always turning attention upon the subconscious whenever the will is being employed.

When acting upon the objective, the will only interferes with normal functions, and can accomplish absolutely nothing. To move a muscle the will must act upon the subconscious life that permeates that muscle; should it act upon the muscle itself, the muscle would become rigid, and muscular motion be made impossible.

No one can do anything by objectively willing to do it; he can do what he wants to do only by causing the will to act upon that part of the subconscious that can do what he wants to have done.

This law is absolute in all human actions, be they physical or metaphysical, intellectual or emotional, mental or spiritual.

To train the will to act only upon the subconscious, will increase the power of the conscious mind to impress the subconscious; the conscious action will not be divided, acting partly upon the objective and partly upon the subjective, but will give its power and attention absolutely to the idea that is being subconsciously impressed.

When the will acts only upon the subconscious, there will be no will force in the outer mind or body to disturb the normal functions of the systems; and when the entire system is normal the subconscious can readily do whatever it may be directed to do.

The conscious mind should employ the will solely for the purpose of impressing and directing the subconscious, but should give the subconscious unrestricted freedom to take full possession of the personality when expressions from within are expected to appear.

Those who hesitate to give the subconscious expressions full right of way, should remember that to move a muscle, the subconscious must take full possession of that muscle; and to think, the subconscious must exercise complete control of the mental faculty, and also, that the subconscious will only do what it is directed to do.

Though the personality must be controlled completely by the subconscious, the subconscious must be directed, in all its actions, by the conscious mind; therefore, the wide-awake self continues to be the master.

Chapter 10

Solutions to Problems

THE subconscious has the power to work out any problem, and find the exact answer to any question, at the time designated by the conscious mind; in fact, no problem is ever worked out by the conscious mind alone; the subconscious gives the real secret in every instance, though it is the conscious mind that makes the practical application.

To secure the direct and the fullest assistance from the subconscious when there are problems to solve, form a clear, distinct idea of what you wish to know, and impress that idea upon the subconscious with a deep, strong desire for the information required. Have perfect faith in the faith that you will receive the answer, and you will.

When you have something special to do at some near future time, that requires more power and mental brilliancy than you usually possess, direct the subconscious to give you the added power and intelligence at the exact time. The subconscious is exact as to time, and will produce, at the time desired, as much power and intelligence as you felt you needed for the special work when the impression was made.

To simply impress upon the subconscious a desire for more power is not sufficient; the impression must contain a clear idea of how much power is required and what the added power is expected to do.

While the subconscious is being impressed for more power, the mind must try to discern and feel the life of more power; and the amount of power that is discerned while the

The Secrets, Mysteries & Powers of The Subconscious Mind
Christian Larson's "The Great Within"

impression is being made, the subconscious will express at the time fixed for the expression.

Whenever an impression is made upon the subconscious, the conscious mind should try to gain the very highest and the very largest conception possible of the idea that is being impressed; and the more clearly the conscious mind discerns the largeness, the worth and the superiority of that idea, the larger, the worthier and the more superior will be the corresponding expression brought forth from the within.

When the conscious mind can see clearly the amount of power and mental brilliancy required for the special future action, and impresses that idea upon the subconscious with the deepest and the strongest desire for its realization, the impression thus made will call for the exact amount of power and intelligence required; and whatever the impression calls for the subconscious will supply.

The law is this, that the subconscious will respond with the exact quality and the exact quantity that you were conscious of, or that you can mentally discern and feel at the time the impression is being made. It is, therefore, extremely important to elevate the conscious mind into the largest and the most superior states of thought and feeling possible before an effort is made to impress the subconscious. In fact, this is the real secret in directing the subconscious to express a larger quantity and a higher quality than we ever received in tangible life before.

To live constantly in the deep, interior feeling of greater power, greater intelligence, greater personal worth and greater mental brilliancy, is to constantly call upon the subconscious to produce these things in larger and larger measure; and the subconscious will invariably do whatever it is called upon to do.

The Secrets, Mysteries & Powers of The Subconscious Mind
Christian Larson's "The Great Within"

Though we should not live in the future in the sense that the mind dwells wholly in the thought of the future, nevertheless, we should always plan ahead.

Place your future plans in the hands of the subconscious; impress upon the subconscious what you wish to have done tomorrow, next week, next month, or even next year; then direct the great within to work out the best plans and the best methods possible, and to give your faculties the understanding and the power to carry out those plans to the most successful termination.

When there is something upon which you cannot decide, inform the subconscious that a definite decision is desired at such and such a time; impress clearly and deeply the facts on all sides concerned, and know that the great within can give the desired decision at the time stated.

When this time comes you will receive your answer through the feeling of a strong, irresistible desire to take one particular course, and that alone.

While the answer is being expected, no anxiety should be felt, even though the last minute should arrive before anything definite appears; the mind that continues in serenity and faith will receive the right answer before it is too late; but the anxious mind will, through the confusion produced by the anxiety, prevent the subconscious from giving expression to the desired information.

When two antagonistic decisions appear at the time fixed, the subconscious expression has not been given full right of way. One of these decisions will be of the conscious mind who judges according to appearances; the other will be of the subconscious who judges according to facts, but which is which may seem difficult to discern.

The Secrets, Mysteries & Powers of The Subconscious Mind
Christian Larson's "The Great Within"

The decision of the conscious mind may sometimes be the stronger, but at other times the weaker; one's strongest feelings, therefore, at such times will not prove to be safe guidance. To re-impress the subconscious for an immediate and a definite decision is the proper course to pursue under such circumstances, and if the conscious mind is kept quiet, in faith, the true answer will shortly appear. You will then feel a strong desire to take but one course, and will lose all desire to even think about the other, because when the subconscious action is given full and free expression, everything that is antagonistic to that expression will cease to exist.

It is therefore evident that we may completely eliminate the wrong by directing the subconscious to express the right, and by giving the subconscious absolute freedom to do what it has been directed to do.

Chapter 11

Direct Assistance in Everything

THE subconscious should be called upon to give direct assistance in everything, even in the most insignificant of everyday affairs; this practice will not only cause all things to be done better and better constantly, but the conscious mind will be more thoroughly trained to impress the subconscious for anything desired, and the subconscious mentality will be perpetually enlarged along all lines.

To enlarge the subconscious mentality in every phase of interior action is to awaken a larger measure of the great within, and the more of the within that is awakened the greater will man become.

For these reasons the subconscious should be called upon for superior aid before anything, even the least, is undertaken. Everything that is worth doing should be done better than before, and the subconscious can provide the power.

Impressions of this nature should be made a few hours in advance, or, when possible, a few days in advance; though the subconscious can respond upon a moment's notice; its superior power should therefore be sought upon every occasion.

In the commercial world no one should ever attempt to decide upon important transactions before directing the subconscious to inspire the mind with the highest insight, the keenest judgment, and the broadest understanding; and no great enterprise should be undertaken before directing

The Secrets, Mysteries & Powers of The Subconscious Mind
Christian Larson's "The Great Within"

the subconscious to work out the best possible plans and methods.

The subconscious can do these things, and when all practical men will go to the greater mind for their plans and ideas, instead of depending upon the limited intelligence of the lesser mind, failures will be reduced to a minimum, while great achievements will steadily increase, both in numbers and in greatness.

Those who are engaged in literary work will find the subconscious indispensable, because any idea desired may be gamed from the great within.

Orators and public speakers should never attempt to prepare or deliver a discourse before going to this great source of ideas for their thought; and the same is true of musical composers, creative artists, inventors, and all others who require ideas that have originality and worth.

Every person who is engaged in study, or in any line of improvement, may increase results from ten to two hundred per cent by securing the direct assistance of the subconscious; and as all advancement and promotion in life comes directly from the improvement of self, the fact that the subconscious can supply any amount of ability, capacity and power, becomes extremely important.

All memory is subconscious, therefore, whatever one desires to remember should be deeply impressed upon the subconscious at the time the fact or idea is received; and the subconscious may be directed to bring back to mind these facts and ideas whenever their recollection is desired.

The Secrets, Mysteries & Powers of The Subconscious Mind
Christian Larson's "The Great Within"

Through this simple process memory can be developed and cultivated to a remarkable degree, and the power to recall anything at any time will become practically perfect.

The subconscious can be trained to keep the conscious mind clear and active, and all sluggishness or obtuseness can be completely eliminated from every faculty. This will enable the student to learn with far greater rapidity, and every mental effort will be conducive to growth.

To produce these results the subconscious should, several times every day, be directed to express continuous clearness, mental lucidity, and a high, well-poised mental activity. While producing that impression, picture in the conscious mind the same clearness and action that you desire the subconscious to express.

To picture perfect lucidity, and to feel high activity in the conscious mind for a few moments while the subconscious is being impressed, will cause the subconscious to express that same clearness and activity for several hours; and when the impression contains a deep desire for greater clearness and activity than the conscious mind can discern, the greater clearness and activity will be expressed.

It is a well-known fact that nearly all great minds, and also most minds that are trying to develop greatness, have moods when they can do most excellent work, but when they are not in those moods little or nothing of worth can be accomplished. To such minds the ability to create the right moods, or mental states, whenever desired, would be of exceptional value, and by properly directing the subconscious it may readily be accomplished.

Form in the conscious mind a very clear idea of the mood or mental state in which you can do your best work, and

The Secrets, Mysteries & Powers of The Subconscious Mind
Christian Larson's "The Great Within"

impress that idea upon the subconscious with a strong desire for the continuous realization of the desired state. Repeat the impression several times every day, and every evening before going to sleep. Perseverance will produce the most remarkable results.

While engaged in any particular study, impress frequently upon the subconscious the real nature of that study, and direct the subconscious to express all the essentials that may be necessary to thoroughly understand and master that study.

Expect superior intelligence from within, and make the best possible use of that intelligence as it is being received. Thus the conscious mind and the subconscious will work together for the promotion of the highest conceivable attainments.

To promote advancement in one's vocation, better plans and methods will constantly be in demand; and by directing the subconscious to work them out these may be secured as required; in addition, the necessary power and ability to practically apply those methods may also be secured if the subconscious is called upon to supply them.

It is the truth that whatever the subconscious is properly impressed and directed to do, it positively will do.

Chapter 12

Make Your Desires Subconscious

TO promote the highest development of mind and soul, a sunny disposition is indispensable; the brighter, the happier and the sweeter the disposition, the more easily and the more rapidly will any talent develop; and it is a literal truth that a sunny disposition is to the talents of the mind what a sunny day is to the flowers of the field.

Every form of disposition comes from the subconscious, be it sweet or otherwise; but the undesirable may be removed completely, and the sweetest and brightest disposition imaginable be permanently established, by daily impressing upon the subconscious your most perfect idea of a sweet and wholesome nature.

As the sweetness of human nature develops, all undesirable feelings and dispositions will disappear; no thought, therefore, should be given to the elimination of perverse characteristics, but the whole of attention should be concentrated upon the development of the wholesome, the sweet and the beautiful.

When there is a tendency to feel out of sorts, turn attention upon the finer side of your nature . . the subconscious . . and think deeply, strongly and feelingly of joy, brightness, kindness, amiableness, cheerfulness, sweetness and loveliness; try to enter into the very life of those states and feel that your entire nature is being recreated in the image and likeness of all that is sweet and beautiful.

The Secrets, Mysteries & Powers of The Subconscious Mind
Christian Larson's "The Great Within"

To permit yourself to feel surly whenever there is a tendency to feel that way is to impress the subconscious with such a state of mind, and the subconscious will respond by giving your nature a stronger tendency to feel surly and out of sorts at the least provocation.

The first indication of ill-feeling in any shape or form should be counteracted at once by immediately directing the subconscious to give expression to the sweet, the wholesome and the beautiful.

It is not only the privilege of every mind to attain greatness, but no mind is doing justice to self that is not doing its utmost to develop greatness; and since a sunny disposition is absolutely necessary to the steady development of ability, talent and genius, neither time nor effort should be spared in recreating the subconscious so completely that every part of its vast domain is permeated through and through with the highest order of human sweetness and mental sunshine.

To recreate the subconscious mentality in the likeness of higher ideals, every impression given to the subconscious should have soul. It is the conscious realization of soul that gives quality, worth and superiority to everything that appears in human life; the reason being that the soul is superiority, and that everything gains superiority that comes in conscious touch with the soul.

To feel soul is to feel the life of real worth, and to impress that feeling upon the subconscious will cause the subconscious to give real worth to every part of the personality.

The Secrets, Mysteries & Powers of The Subconscious Mind
Christian Larson's "The Great Within"

The subconscious should be directed daily to give worth and superiority to the entire being of man; and this is positively can do.

The great within should be directed to work for greater things, and when every impression is impressed in the feeling of soul, every impression will cause the within to unfold, develop and give expression to greater things.

All greatness comes from the awakening of the great within; to awaken the great within is to feel greatness, and to be filled with the power that is greatness . . the power that will invariably produce greatness.

Ability, talent and genius of the highest order must inevitably follow the development of the great within; likewise, the strong mind, the invincible character and the beautiful soul. Every faculty increases in power, capacity and quality as its subconscious side is being developed, and this subconscious side may be developed by concentrating attention upon the interior, finer essence of that faculty while the most perfect idea or conception of that faculty is held in mind.

The development of the subconscious side of the entire personality will increase the drawing power of the personality, the power that attracts both directly and indirectly, whatever the mind may desire.

This power is the result of subconscious action, and therefore increases, both in volume and in natural attraction, as a greater measure of the within is awakened.

There are many personalities that are strong, but that do not attract, while there are many others that lack in power but that are very attractive in proportion to the power they do possess. The cause of the former condition is an awakened subconscious life that does not receive free and orderly expression; the cause of the latter condition is a limited subconscious life that is not disturbed nor hindered in its expression.

To steadily increase subconscious action and give that action a well-poised expression will cause the personality to become practically irresistible in its power of attraction.

The drawing power of the subconscious lies in its ability, not only to give extraordinary power to the personality, but also to produce ideas that draw, plans that draw, methods that draw and systems that draw.

It is not only ideas, but the way those ideas are arranged, that determines results; and it is not only high-class work, but the way that work is presented, that determines the measure of success. The best ideas may be ignored completely by the world, and the best work may have to be abandoned through the lack of appreciation, and the subconscious life that is expressed through those ideas or efforts is at fault.

Direct the subconscious not only to give you the best ideas, the best plans and the best methods, but also direct the subconscious to give the proper expression to those ideas and methods. When the proper expression is made the attention of the world will be attracted; your ideas will be understood, the real worth of your work will be appreciated, and your efforts will be in constant demand.

The subconscious can work out the best ideas and create the best expression of those ideas; it can give the power and the ability to do greater things, and can give your work that

The Secrets, Mysteries & Powers of The Subconscious Mind
Christian Larson's "The Great Within"

mysterious something that will attract both the attention and the appreciation of the world.

The subconscious in every mind should therefore be directed to do these things, because no person is just to himself who does not make the best use of everything that exists in his nature.

The subconscious, when so directed, will give a natural drawing power to all the finer thought currents; these in turn will convey the same qualities to every part of the mentality and the personality; this will cause everything that man is, and everything that he does, to be stamped with that something that attracts attention and commands appreciation; his desires will consequently become irresistible.

The desires of such a mind will have the power to create their own way to their own goal, no matter how lofty that goal may be. The power of the subconscious is limitless, therefore, nothing becomes impossible when we awaken the great within.

All desires should be made subconscious, and when those desires are constantly expressed with the deepest feeling and the strongest desire that can possibly be aroused, you will positively receive what you want. If it fails to come through one channel it will come through another; but come it will, because the subconscious has the power to do whatever it is directed to do.

To subconsciously desire something is to make yourself strong enough and able enough to command, create or attract that something.

The Secrets, Mysteries & Powers of The Subconscious Mind
Christian Larson's "The Great Within"

Make your desires subconscious and the subconscious will make you worthy of what you desire; the subconscious desire will awaken the same quality and worth in yourself that already exists in that which you desire, and, as like does attract like, you will invariably get what you desire when you become equal to what you desire.

The subconscious desire for abundance will develop in yourself the power to earn and create abundance; it will increase your earning capacity, and will, both directly and indirectly, change your personality so that you will be naturally drawn into environments and associations where you can make the best possible use of that increase of capacity.

The subconscious, being limitless, can work out ideas and plans that you can use in your present position in furthering your desire for the better position; the subconscious, if directed, will find a way; especially so if the desire is very deep and very strong; and you will also receive the power and the ability to do whatever that way may demand.

It is therefore evident that whatever a person's conditions or circumstances may be today, the subconscious can, and will, open the door to something better, providing there is a strong subconscious desire for something better.

Chapter 13

Produce Perfect Health

TO awaken the great within is to awaken to a universe of higher attainments, greater achievements and more far-reaching possibilities than one has ever dreamed of before; it is to enter that world where every desire will be granted, every aspiration realized and every ideal fulfilled.

To promote this awakening, direct the subconscious to give its best to every thought and every action, and when this best has been received, direct the subconscious to produce something still better. It can; the subconscious can do whatever we may wish to have done. Every condition that appears in the body, be it favorable or otherwise, comes either directly or indirectly from the subconscious; that is, it may be the direct effect of a corresponding subconscious cause, or it may be the effect of external causes that were permitted to act upon the body because the true subconscious expression was absent.

No external cause can produce disease in the body so long as the subconscious is giving a full expression to perfect health; and no curative agent from the without can restore health in the body so long as the subconscious is giving expression to diseased conditions.

The majority of physical ills can be cured by nature when the subconscious ceases to give expression to weakening and disease producing conditions, and all diseases can be permanently removed by training the subconscious to give a full and constant expression of health.

The Secrets, Mysteries & Powers of The Subconscious Mind
Christian Larson's "The Great Within"

Personal and physical conditions are effects; they are caused either directly or indirectly by the subconscious; therefore, any condition desired in the personality may be produced through the proper direction of the subconscious.

To direct the subconscious to produce perfect health, the first essential is to gain a clear conscious realization of the state of perfect health, and the second essential is to permeate the subconscious with this realization.

The subconscious mind is a deeper and a finer state of mental life that exists within every atom of the human system; it is another mental world, so to speak, and is so immense that the ordinary conscious mind is mere insignificance in comparison. But it obeys perfectly the directions of the conscious mind, and, having limitless power in every part of the body, can readily banish any disease when properly directed to do so.

To impress the subconscious, attention should be concentrated upon this superior mental world, and all thought should be gradually refined until one can feel that the conscious thought has been completely transformed into the spiritual fineness of the subconscious thought.

The subconscious may be reached most directly by concentrating upon the brain center, though attention must not be fixed upon the physical brain, but upon that finer mental life that permeates the physical brain.

All general directions given to the subconscious should be given through the brain center, but for the curing of physical ailments attention should be concentrated upon the subconscious mentality that permeates the organ, muscle or nerve where the ailment is located.

The Secrets, Mysteries & Powers of The Subconscious Mind
Christian Larson's "The Great Within"

To impress the conscious realization of health upon the subconscious life of any part of the body will cause the subconscious to bring forth into that part of the body the same condition of health which the conscious mind realized while the impression was being made; it is, therefore, necessary to attain the very highest possible conscious understanding of the real state of perfect health before the subconscious is directed to produce health.

No thought of disease should form in mind while the subconscious is being impressed with perfect health; neither should one think of the body. To think of the body is to form mental conceptions of the way physical conditions now feel, and if these conditions are undesirable, undesirable impressions will enter the subconscious, to be followed by the formation of more undesirable conditions in the near future.

The imperfection of physical conditions should never enter mind at any time, because such conditions are liable to be deeply felt, and whatever is deeply felt will be impressed upon the subconscious, whether we so wish or no; neither should there be any desire to remove or overcome that which may seem undesirable. To desire to remove the wrong is to deeply think about the wrong, because all desires tend to deepen the actions of thought, and to deeply think about the wrong is to impress the wrong upon the subconscious. It is sowing weeds in the fields of the mind, and the harvest will be accordingly.

All thought should be animated with the consciousness of that perfection in health and wholeness that we desire to realize in expression, and all feeling should be trained to feel the health, the life and the harmony that the subconscious is being directed to produce. To consciously live through and through the finer subconscious mentality for a few moments, several times every day, and deeply impress one's most perfect realization of health upon the entire subconscious mentality will cause the subconscious to give a full and constant expression of health.

The result will be perpetual health, without a moment of any form of sickness at any time, and if the conscious mind will seek to daily impress upon the subconscious a more and more perfect realization of absolute health, the subconscious will steadily improve the quality of the health that is being expressed.

To eliminate a local ailment the subconscious mentality that permeates that part of the body should be impressed with the conscious feeling of the health that is desired.

Concentrate upon the finer mental life in that part of the body where the adverse condition appears and feel the reality of perfect health. Do not concentrate upon the physical organ, nor even think of the physical organ, but enter mentally into the interior subconscious life of that organ and, while in that state, feel the spirit of perfect health with all the depth of mind and soul.

What you feel, while in that state, you impress upon the subconscious, and the subconscious will cause perfect health to be expressed through every atom of that organ.

To eliminate a chronic ailment, impress perfect health upon the subconscious as a whole, while concentrating upon the subconscious mentality within the brain center. Also concentrate frequently upon the subconscious side of the entire personality, feeling the state of perfect health in the subconscious life of every part of the system.

The Secrets, Mysteries & Powers of The Subconscious Mind
Christian Larson's "The Great Within"

If certain parts of the body are specially affected, impress those parts in the same way as for a local ailment, though local attention should be given, not so much to those parts of the body that feel the effects of the ailment as to those parts where the adverse condition has its origin. Before impressing the subconscious the entire system should be made as calm and peaceful as possible, and the principal directions should be given to the subconscious immediately before going to sleep.

The most important of all, however, is to live, think and act in the absolute faith that the subconscious can and will do whatever it is directed to do.

Chapter 14

Impress the Subconscious Before Sleep

DURING the waking state the conscious ego acts directly upon the conscious, or wide awake mind, while during sleep it acts entirely in the subconscious.

When we go to sleep all the principal thoughts, desires, intentions, tendencies, feelings and ideas that have formed during the day are taken into the subconscious, unless we eliminate the undesirable mental material before we permit sleep to take place.

Every thought, desire, idea that is taken into the subconscious as mind falls asleep will be impressed upon the subconscious, and will cause corresponding expressions to be brought forth into the personality. To eliminate all undesirable thoughts and feelings from mind before going to sleep is therefore extremely important.

Before going to sleep the conscious mind should be thoroughly cleansed from everything that one does not care to reproduce or perpetuate, and the subconscious should be given definite directions as to what should be developed, reproduced and expressed.

The hours of sleep may be employed in the development of anything we may have in view, because whatever we impress upon mind when we go to sleep will enter the subconscious and will cause the within to give expression to those effects that we desire to secure in the without.

The Secrets, Mysteries & Powers of The Subconscious Mind
Christian Larson's "The Great Within"

Before going to sleep the subconscious should be given full directions as to what is to be done in the near future, and the exact time for each particular action should be specified as far as possible. In the meantime the subconscious will work out the best plans, methods and ideas, and provide the added understanding, insight and power required to apply those plans in the most effective manner.

When the subconscious is properly directed in this way the results from future actions may be increased to a degree that will frequently be remarkable, and, as much produces more, these results will follow the law of perpetual increase.

During the waking state the mind forms a definite conception of everything that is given real, conscious attention; these conceptions individualize themselves into ideas and as mind goes to sleep all those ideas are taken into the subconscious.

Therefore, what the subconscious is given to work out and develop during sleep will depend upon what we think about during the day, and what we give the subconscious to develop and express will determine what character, mentality and personality are to be.

The subconscious makes us what we are, in every respect, but what the subconscious is to make will depend upon what our thoughts, feelings and desires may direct.

The more we think during the day, providing our thought has quality, the more good seeds we shall place in the garden of the mind during sleep, and the greater will be the quality and the quantity of the coming harvest.

The Secrets, Mysteries & Powers of The Subconscious Mind
Christian Larson's "The Great Within"

The stronger our desires for wisdom, power, attainments and achievements during the waking state, the more thoroughly will the subconscious work for those things during sleep. The subconscious can provide all the essentials required for the highest attainments and greatest achievements and will do so if directed.

The subconscious works during sleep, and works to develop the ideas and the desires that the conscious mind brought into the subconscious while falling asleep, but the subconscious will give the same attention to ideas and desires that are detrimental, just as rich soil will apply the same productiveness to the weed as to the Sower.

It is therefore wisdom to sow good seeds only; to eliminate all undesirable thought, ideas and feelings before sleep begins.

The habit of going to sleep every night with all sorts of thoughts in mind is the principal cause of the continuous mingling of good and evil in the life of the average person. The troubles and the worries of the day are taken into the subconscious at night, along with those thoughts and feelings that have better things in view, and the subconscious, consequently, continues to work for more good things on the one hand and for more troubles and worries on the other. It is the truth that any person may emancipate himself completely from all the ills of perverted life by refusing absolutely to permit a single undesirable thought, feeling or desire to enter the subconscious.

To prevent the wrong from entering the subconscious we must, during the waking state, never think, with feeling, of that which is evil, imperfect or wrong, and before going to sleep the conscious mind must be cleansed completely from every undesirable thought or impression that may have entered unconsciously during the day.

The imperfect will not impress itself upon the subconscious during the waking state unless we think about it in deep feeling, but everything that is in the conscious mind when we go to sleep will enter the subconscious and produce fruit after its kind.

To cleanse the conscious mind before going to sleep, enter a state of perfect mental poise; be still in the deepest sense of the term; forget what you do not wish to retain by entering into the very life and essence of that which you desire to awaken, unfold and develop. Then concentrate upon the subconscious with the deepest possible feeling and the strongest possible desire.

What you wish to remove from mind may be removed by directing the subconscious to create and express the opposite, though no thought should be given to that which is not to be retained. When you know what you wish to remove, forget it by giving your entire subconscious attention to that which you wish to create and realize instead.

To carry into the subconscious those ideas that we wish to develop is not all that is necessary, however, as we go to sleep; the subconscious should be given the best possible conditions in which to work.

The subconscious is in close touch with all the functions of the body as well as the actions of the mind, therefore, the entire system must be in harmony and order before sleep begins or subconscious action will be confused and misdirected.

The Secrets, Mysteries & Powers of The Subconscious Mind
Christian Larson's "The Great Within"

Before going to sleep the body should be in harmony, the mind in peace an d the entire personality relaxed. The circulation should be even, and no part should be too warm nor too cold. Digestion should be practically finished and there should be nothing in the system that might disturb any of the functions during sleep.

When physical functions are disturbed during sleep the conscious ego is drawn back to the outer mind, either fully or in part, and its work in the subconscious is interrupted. Such interruptions usually misdirect the subconscious actions to such an extent that the very opposite results to what were intended are produced.

This explains why such detrimental results are frequently secured, even when our intentions were the best and our plans carried out with the greatest of care. It also proves that the entire system must be kept in order if every action, conscious or subconscious, is to produce the results desired.

Chapter 15

Sleeping on Difficult Problems

WHEN the conscious ego, which is you, yourself, enters the subconscious during sleep, there are two objects in view. The first object is to carry into the subconscious the new ideas that have formed during the day and the second object is to recharge the system with life, power and energy.

The subconscious supplies the life and the energy that is required to perpetuate the existence of the mentality and the personality, but to receive this energy the conscious ego must enter the subconscious, and should remain there, uninterruptedly, for six or seven hours out of every twenty-four, to secure the full measure of power. When sleep is interrupted the personality does not receive as much life as may be required to keep the system in the fullest and most perfect action; personal efforts will, therefore, become inferior.

When all the conditions are provided for properly recuperating and recharging the system during sleep, and the subconscious is directed to steadily increase the supply of power, the personality will become stronger and more vigorous from year to year; instead of going down to weakness and age the personality will go on to greater strength, greater capacity, greater ability and greater power the longer you live.

To go to sleep properly is to wake up feeling refreshed, but to go to sleep with all sorts of impressions in the mind and all sorts of conditions in the body is to wake up feeling stupid and depressed.

The Secrets, Mysteries & Powers of The Subconscious Mind
Christian Larson's "The Great Within"

To enter the subconscious with adverse impressions is to return to consciousness with similar conditions. Like causes always produce like effects.

To aid the mind in purifying itself before going to sleep, attention should be concentrated upon the purest purity and the highest worth that can possibly be imagined, and to place the entire system in a state of peace, concentrate the thought of peace upon the brain center while gently drawing all the finer forces of mind toward that center.

To think, with feeling, of the finer forces of mind during this process will produce immediate results.

The practice of "sleeping over" difficult problems before definite decisions are made is a practice of great value, especially when the subconscious is properly directed in the matter, because the subconscious can "turn things over" more completely during sleep than during the waking state.

To secure the best results hold clearly and serenely in mind the elements involved in the problem just as you are going to sleep and desire deeply, but without anxiety, to receive the correct answer upon awakening.

The higher and the clearer the conception that is formed of the problem during the waking state the more readily can the subconscious work it out during sleep. The same is true in the various ideas that are formed during the day and that are taken into the great within either at sleep or during waking states of deep feeling.

It is therefore extremely important to form the highest possible conception of everything that we think of during the day, and whatever attracts our attention should be considered from the very highest point of view.

The Secrets, Mysteries & Powers of The Subconscious Mind
Christian Larson's "The Great Within"

Live in the upper story of mind and give soul to all your thought; you will thereby form ideas with real quality and worth, and as those ideas are taken into the subconscious during sleep they will cause greater quality and worth to be developed in you.

No person can afford to take a commonplace view of anything, nor to indulge in cheap thinking at any time; to do so is to place inferior seeds in the garden of the mind.

There are days when the average person feels as if he amounted to practically nothing; his personality lacks energy and his mind is dull, stupid and confused. Cheap, superficial thinking a day or two before is the cause.

Give inferior ideas to the subconscious, and the subconscious will, in the near future, not only cause you to feel incompetent and inferior, but your mind will temporarily be placed in a state where it actually becomes incompetent and inferior.

To produce worthy ideas it is not necessary to always continue in profound or serious states of mind; the thought of worth is the thought that mind creates while attention dwells in the life of quality and soul, and while consciousness is thoroughly permeated with the desire to realize quality and soul in everything.

Such thinking can be taken into all thought and all life, even into every pleasure. To try to enjoy pleasures while mind skims over the surface of life and thought is to fail to receive the joy that is joy, or the satisfaction that does satisfy; but when pleasures are entered into with the feeling of quality and finer life, even the simplest of joys become founts of supreme joy.

The Secrets, Mysteries & Powers of The Subconscious Mind
Christian Larson's "The Great Within"

Everything that we thoroughly enjoy we impress upon the subconscious; therefore, to enter into pleasure while mind is in the attitude of cheapness or inferiority is a mistake to be avoided under every circumstance.

However, our pleasures may be used as channels through which the subconscious may be impressed and directed along lines of superior attainment, and pleasures that are employed in this manner will invariably give the greatest, the most satisfying and the most wholesome joy of all joys.

Chapter 16

Sleep on the Superior; The Ideal

THE entire human personality is being constantly renewed; there is nothing about mind or body that can possibly become old, except the appearance, and the appearance of age is caused by a wrong subconscious process.

The process of perpetual renewal is carried on by the subconscious, but it is what the conscious mind gives to the subconscious that determines both the quality and the appearance of the personality.

To constantly give the subconscious better ideas, better desires, better thoughts and better mental states is to cause the improvement of character, mentality and personality to become perpetual.

To provide better material for the subconscious, the conscious mind, before going to sleep, should eliminate everything but those ideas, thoughts and desires that have quality and worth, and every effort should be made during the waking state to form the most superior ideas possible on every subject with which the mind may come in contact.

Never go to sleep discouraged, nor with the thought of failure in mind. To fear failure while going to sleep is to impress the subconscious with the idea of failure, and the subconscious will respond by producing conditions in the system that are failures; the system will, consequently, fail to be its best, and will lose ground, more and more, until real failure takes place.

The Secrets, Mysteries & Powers of The Subconscious Mind
Christian Larson's "The Great Within"

To go to sleep discouraged, disappointed, worried or depressed, is to impress the subconscious with weakening tendencies; these will cause the subconscious to express conditions of weakness in every faculty and in every part of mind or body.

The tendency downward in any career originates invariably in depressed subconscious states, the majority of which are taken into the subconscious as the mind goes to sleep. Every tendency upward and onward toward higher attainments and greater achievements, originates in constructive subconscious states and it is possible for anyone to produce such states at will.

By going to sleep with strong, clear ideas of health, harmony, power, advancement and success, clearly held in mind, the causes of those things will be formed in the subconscious and the effects will invariably appear in external life. Your health will at once begin to improve; more power will appear in mind and body; capacity will increase; all your talents and faculties will be filled with the spirit of success, and will consequently, do far better work than ever before.

To continue, for weeks and months, the practice of giving superior ideas of all kinds to the subconscious, upon going to sleep, will cause the character, the mentality and the personality to improve to such an extent that, in comparison with your former self, you will actually become a superior being.

When the subconscious is given something special to do every night sleep will become more restful; the subconscious always works during sleep, but will work more orderly when given something definite to do.

The Secrets, Mysteries & Powers of The Subconscious Mind
Christian Larson's "The Great Within"

After the subconscious has been properly directed no anxiety should be felt as to results; perfect faith in the law, with that quiet assurance that knows, will give the law the proper conditions through which the desired results can be produced.

When we go to sleep in states of discord the mental material becomes confused and incoherent mental formations are produced; these are sometimes remembered as disagreeable dreams.

All such formations are produced by confusion among the subconscious creative energies and indicate that the true state of sleep was not entered completely, also that the subconscious was not properly impressed the night before.

Orderly and coherent dreams may indicate what tendencies are at work in the subconscious and whether desirable or undesirable conditions are being formed, because a dream is always a partial memory of what is taking place in the subconscious.

By noting this fact, undesirable conditions may be counteracted and removed before they advance sufficiently to produce tangible results.

An undesirable dream should always be counteracted at once by impressing the opposite, desirable conditions and qualities upon the subconscious; tendencies, however, that are indicated in good dreams, should be given added power. This can be done by directing the subconscious to work more thoroughly for the promotion of the greater good at hand.

Every good dream is a prophecy; that is, it indicates what the subconscious can do, what it is ready to do, or what it is about to do along certain lines, and this prophecy can be made to come true by directing the subconscious to proceed along those lines with greater power and determination than ever before.

These directions should be given to the subconscious as frequently as possible during the waking state, as well as before going to sleep.

Every desirable indication among the greater, interior life forces, whether it be discovered through dreams or intuition, should be taken advantage of at once, and all the forces of mind should be concentrated upon the goal that the vision has placed within reach; a successful termination will invariably be the result; the dream will come true, the prophecy will be fulfilled, the ideal will be realized.

Chapter 17

Awaking the Great Within

THE subconscious mind is not a second mind; to think so is to place an artificial barrier between the outer person and the limitless within. There is but one mind; the outer phase is the conscious or the objective; the inner phase is the subconscious or the subjective. The subconscious is within the conscious, and, being unlimited, both in power and in possibilities, is appropriately termed the great within.

To awaken the great within is to bring into action the powers and the possibilities that are latent in the subconscious, and since the powers of the within are limitless, and its possibilities numberless, this awakening may be promoted indefinitely, increasing without end the worth and the greatness of man.

The awakening of the great within is promoted directly through a perpetual increase of conscious action upon the subconscious, and the power of the conscious mind to act upon the subconscious will increase in proportion to the practical use that is made of every added expression that appears from the within.

The fact that the within is limitless, and the fact that the greatness of the within can be brought forth into expression in greater and greater measure through the proper action of the conscious mind upon the subconscious proves conclusively that man may become as great as he may desire to be, and that his ability, his talent and his genius may be developed, not only to a most remarkable degree, but to any degree.

The Secrets, Mysteries & Powers of The Subconscious Mind
Christian Larson's "The Great Within"

Personally, each person is only as much as he has, consciously or unconsciously, directed the subconscious to produce, and he will remain what he is so long as he does not direct the subconscious to produce more; but he may become more, as much more as his highest aspiration can picture, by awakening the great within.

To train the conscious mind to act upon the subconscious with the greatest efficiency, a clear idea of how the two phases of mind are related to each other becomes necessary, and this idea is readily understood when we realize that mind is an immense sea of soul forces, all of which move in circles and spirals.

The circumference of each circle is acted upon by the conscious ego during the waking state, therefore, the sum total of all the circumferences of all the mental circles may be termed the outer mind, the objective mind, the conscious mind, the wide-awake mind.

During sleep the conscious ego withdraws from the circumference of the mental circles and enters the mental field within; that is, the subconscious.

While the mind is in state of deep feeling the conscious ego acts partly upon the conscious side of mind and partly upon the subconscious; it is possible, therefore, while in that state, to impress upon the subconscious what we think or feel in the conscious.

To secure the best and the largest results from every mental action the conscious ego should, during the waking state, act constantly both upon the conscious and the subconscious. To be in constant touch with the limitless powers of the within will add remarkably to the capacity as well as the quality of the faculties that may be in use, and

The Secrets, Mysteries & Powers of The Subconscious Mind
Christian Larson's "The Great Within"

every conscious desire will enter the subconscious at once, so that an immediate response may be secured, if required. The strong mind is the mind that is in such close touch with the great within that the limitless powers of the within can be felt at any tune.

The capacity of such a mind will be practically unbounded; weariness will be absent; mental brilliancy will ever be on the increase, and instead of going down with the years, as the average mind does, such a mind will steadily advance in higher attainments and greater achievements the longer the person may live.

The mind that has presence of mind at all times, and under all circumstances, is in perfect touch with the subconscious. In fact, if the subconscious is impressed every day, or better still, several times a day, to guide the outer mind so perfectly that the right step will always be taken at the right time, the conscious mind will intuitively know what to do to secure the best results from every circumstance, action or event.

When the powers of the subconscious are realized one's ideas will become much higher than before, and there will be a tendency to form ideals that cannot be realized with present states of development, but since the proper direction of the subconscious can promote development to any degree desired, it is not justice to self to remain content with the lesser while the greater is in view.

However, no desire should be entertained that cannot be fulfilled through the complete application of present ability, nor should present demands go beyond what present capacity is known to be.

The Secrets, Mysteries & Powers of The Subconscious Mind
Christian Larson's "The Great Within"

The proper course is to first increase the capacity, then desire what the increased capacity has the power to fulfill.

The small mind must not desire the realization of ideals that the great mind alone can possibly make real; such a course would be a waste of time; it would be schooling oneself to desire only what cannot be secured, while doing nothing to so increase one's power that the object in view could easily be secured.

The subconscious can make the small mind great, as great as may be necessary to realize any ideal, but greatness does not come from dreaming about the ideal, nor from concentrating upon that which is beyond our present capacity to produce.

Develop greatness by awakening the great within, and that power that can produce anything and realize anything will be gained.

Development is gradual and does not simply consist in the unfoldment of added power and capacity, but also in the full tangible use of that power and capacity.

To proceed orderly toward greatness direct the subconscious to express what may be necessary to take the next step forward; concentrate all the forces of mind upon that step, and do not scatter mind over realms and spheres that are beyond that step; do now what you are doing now, and be satisfied to realize what can be realized now.

Proceed with the second step in the same way and, likewise, with the innumerable steps that are to follow.

This is true progress; it is concentrating the whole of attention upon the present advancement, and there is no other advancement. To move forward we must advance in the present, and in the present only.

To move forward now is the purpose, and he who continues to move forward now will reach any goal he may have in view.

The subconscious should, therefore, be directed to turn all its superior powers upon the present forward movement and should be daily impressed to desire, not the ideals of the distant future, but the ideals that can be realized today.

This forward movement, however, should not be confined to any one phase of existence; all things in the physical, the metaphysical and the spiritual nature of man should be developed simultaneously and perpetually.

It is the greatness of everything in man that gives man the greatness that is greatness, and the perpetual awakening of the great within will produce this greatness, because to the powers and the possibilities of the great within there is no limit, neither is there any end.

The End

Metaphysical / Law of Attraction Books

David Allen - The Power of I AM (2014), The Power of I AM - Volume 2 (2015) , The Power of I AM - Volume 3 (2017)

David Allen - The Creative Power of Thought, Man's Greatest Discovery (2017)

David Allen - The Secrets, Mysteries & Powers of The Subconscious Mind (2017)

David Allen - The Money Bible - The Secrets of Attracting Prosperity (2017)

David Allen - Your Faith Is Your Fortune, Your Unlimited Power

The Neville Goddard Collection (All 10 of his books plus 2 Lecture series) (2016)

Neville Goddard - Assumptions Harden Into Facts: The Book (2016)

Neville Goddard - Imagination: The Redemptive Power in Man (2016)

Neville Goddard - The World is At Your Command - The Very Best of Neville Goddard (2017)

Neville Goddard - Imagining Creates Reality - 365 Mystical Daily Quotes (2017)

Neville Goddard's Interpretation of Scripture (2018)

The Definitive Christian D. Larson Collection (6 Volumes, 30 books) (2014)

Notes:

The Secrets, Mysteries & Powers of The Subconscious Mind

Notes:

www.ingramcontent.com/pod-product-compliance
Lightning Source LLC
Chambersburg PA
CBHW021122300426
44113CB00006B/249